FIERY FAITH
A MESSAGE TO ALL

REBEKAH ACQUAH

Fiery FAITH

Copyright © 2024 by Rebekah Acquah.

All rights reserved. No part of this publication may be reproduced, distributed, or transmitted in any form or by any means, including photocopying, recording, or other electronic or mechanical methods, without the written consent of the publisher. The only exceptions are for brief quotations included in critical reviews and other noncommercial uses permitted by copyright law.

MILTON & HUGO L.L.C.
4407 Park Ave., Suite 5
Union City, NJ 07087, USA

Website: *www. miltonandhugo.com*
Hotline: *1- 888-778-0033*
Email: *info@miltonandhugo.com*

Ordering Information:
Quantity sales. Special discounts are granted to corporations, associations, and other organizations. For more information on these discounts, please reach out to the publisher using the contact information provided above.

Library of Congress Control Number: 2024927057
ISBN-13:   979-8-89285-397-2   [Paperback Edition]
           979-8-89285-398-9   [Digital Edition]

Rev. date: 12/19/2024

Contents

Acknowledgments vii
Introduction ix
Author's Message xi
Chapter 1   Crazy, Undeniable Faith 1
Chapter 2   Words 13
Chapter 3   All Seasons 31
Chapter 4   Obedience 37
Chapter 5   The Shoulder of a Strong Source 43
Chapter 6   Others 47
Chapter 7   Thoughts of Peace 53
Chapter 8   Two Faith Aligned 59
Chapter 9   What We Hear 65
Chapter 10 Fiery Faith Moments of Others 73
Reference 95

Acknowledgments

The men and women who have toil tirelessly and feel that they have not been heard by others and, most importantly, by God!

The boys and girls who at times endlessly feel no one is listening to their youthful cries and real struggles.

To the weary individual who needs just one confirmation that they are doing the right thing!

To the individual who perceives that they are living in and by faith and perhaps needs some confirmation.

Allow this book of true moments in faith to be that help you have longed for.

May it guide you and give you hope when things appear to be hopeless.

Keep on pushing to your own testimony of your *fiery faith*.

Now it's time.

Turn the pages...

Introduction

This book is filled with experiences of true, real-time events.

> Truly I tell you, if you have faith as small as a mustard seed, you can say to this mountain, "Move from here to there," and it will move. Nothing will be impossible for you. (Matthew 17:20 NIV)

> Faith is trusting in the pilot that flies the plane you are in with no question to your destination.

Author's Message

Picture yourself with a small key that opens up the place you live. Now you go and stand at the door and shout very loud, "I believe when I open this door, I will enter this place and be safe. I will eat, sleep, and be happy. I believe this."

Okay, now one-hour passes, and you are still at the door. Two hours…and so on. Now it's getting to nighttime, and it's getting cold. You are becoming hungrier by the minute. You finally decide to act on what you believe with your mind and what you shouted out; and you insert the key into the door, turn the key, push the door, then open the door with the key you believed and knew would open the door.

If you would have kept believing and shouting but not acting on what you were saying, you would have remained at believe and not faith. You would have remained out there and possibly froze to death with a hungry stomach.

Every day we utilize these two things in our lives whether you are a believer of the gospel of Christ Jesus or not. We live out our faith consistently without knowing it. What leads to the crazy and fiery part? Now, that takes more.

Here is another: Water and fire have sources. In order to shut a waterfall from flowing, you must find the source where you can shut it from. In the same way, fire has a source, and in order to stop a fire from burning up everything in its way, you need to find the source, then you water the source of the fire to quench it faster. On the other hand, water can dry up eventually, if the source is not running. Yet the dryness can still be recovered once the source is revived again. This phenomenon is what differs water from fire, although they are both powerful in their own way.

Fire, in itself, once it is let loose to burn, recovery to its initial state cannot be revived.

So like fire and water, the topic of faith is similar, where you must understand and know what is the source your faith id deriving from. Meanwhile, a fiery faith holds a stronger foundation in the metaphoric comparison.

Once your faith is lit up, breathing life attached to the source, it cannot go back to its initial state (excluding having a traumatic brain injury and other medical reasons that affects memory traumatically)! Like fire that once burns an item, the evidence remains that you have been touched by the source of faith! A seed has been planted whether you watered it or not. Of course, if it is not water, it has a higher chance of withering away in a shorter span. Meanwhile, there will remain evidence and a subconscious remembrance of the seed that was planted in your mind and your heart, even in some cases of a traumatic brain injury.

Here's another metaphoric example to insist on an understanding before continuing: A baby that is born cannot be unborn once the birthing has occurred. Even as small as the child may be at the very minute of birth, it cannot return to its mother's womb. This baby came from one seed of implantation.

When a seed is implanted to make a baby, the originals of that seed are the parents, but when the child is born, the child does not look 100 percent like the parents, despite the deoxyribonucleic acid (DNA) having a 100 percent confirmation that those are the child's parents. Even if the child looks like the parents, there are differences in the resemblance. Just like fire wherein the ashes says that there has been a fire. The original state was there, but once it's been touched by the fire, to go back to the original state in the very same way it was birthed is impossible. This type of faith becomes *fiery faith*, a faith that can never return to its original state from whence it was birthed. Fire is important in this concept regarding faith, because whether your faith remains as a mustard-seed faith, grows, or withers, fire is the emblem of revival. In plain English, fire is a symbolic representation needed to improve and strengthen your faith to a new *fiery awakening*. Hence, after reading this book, a congratulation is in place, and I welcome you in advance to the family of a source of fiery faith.

Chapter

1

Crazy, Undeniable Faith

THE BELIEVER: *Aaaachhuu!*
THE ATHEIST: God bless you.

> If you do not stand firm in your faith, you will not stand at all. (Isaiah 7:9)

Have you had a realization where you think you must be crazy?

Okay, if you have had this realization at some point, good, let's continue.

If you have not had such a moment, it's okay. Imagination is important in the world we live in, so let's still continue this journey.

Imagine everyone else around you seems to be living in a different world than you, where your reality seems to be estranged. Okay, let me make sense of this. You are having a moment where what comes out of your mouth genuinely makes others feel you are not living in reality (it probably makes them cringe, and some might be concerned about your mental state). An example: Some may say, "How can you believe certain things will happen when your physical present situation is far from what you speak of happening in your life or those around you?" A moment where even you can see that what is coming out of your mouth is far from what your reality is. Then you realize in this same moment that this is not just being spoken from your mouth, you truly believe in this miraculous thing happening. From the depths of your heart, it has been engraved. You cannot explain it physically in that moment, but you just know what you are saying will happen, that it will realistically come to fruition. For example, saying, "I will retire in ten years," when the retirement age is sixty-five and you are literally still in your twenties. Or perhaps saying, "I will not pay student loans in this country," while you owe over $100,000.00 in student loans. How about this one? When your credit score is literally not yet in the 700s, and you say to a friend that you will purchase a new home in *cash*. Wait, what about this? When looking at your account, it does not seem so with a $150.00 balance. Yeah, I chuckled at that last one as well.

So you are either at this point just plain in denial of your reality, or you're just simply crazy? Because you are not someone who is lucky nor do you believe in luck.

But wait, how about a third option? An option that is seemingly fading in the background of today's world, in the twenty-first century. An option that is becoming a fear of discussion. One that was once at the no. 1 spot but is slowly diminishing. A third and very valid third option that says, "No, you are not *crazy*." Well, maybe a little. In fact, you probably have to be crazy to believe this option and step out of the five physical senses to see that this option may be the first real choice to what you are experiencing. This option has evidence and has proven itself in the medical field to keep others alive longer and also provide psychiatric healing. An investigation by David H. Rosmarin, a Harvard medical school instructor and a clinician in the department of psychiatry at McLean stated, "Harnessing spiritual resources in treatment may lead to lower suicide rates and better treatment outcomes for psychiatric patients." Yet to go further, the power of the words that we profess from the heart matters. The studies showed that those who were religious and blamed God or the devil for their sickness and became bitter had a lower chance of their healing as compared to similarly religious patients who professed positively God's plan and spoke healing words. They are more likely to be healed (O'Brien 2013). This third option, which fits best as the first option is faith. Faith has both medical and psychological evidence that has shown itself to be a key player in mental and physical health stability. In my profession as a therapist, I have seen this in many of my clients. The ones who reported having a spiritual belief, specifically in God the creator of the heavens and Earth became mentally stable sooner than those who are only relying on themselves for better mental status and to cure their self-esteem. So let me be the first to tell you that you may not be in denial, you may not be simply crazy. Hence, the word "simply." Could it be what you are experiencing is faith? Not just faith, but crazy, undeniable faith?

Let this word sink in for a moment before reading on faith, crazy, undeniable faith.

So, what is this thing called faith? Before we move on, it is important to define this for understanding purposes, which removes any assumptions we may have.

The Oxford dictionary states faith is when we have complete trust or confidence in someone or something. Believers would define it as a strong belief in God or in the doctrines of a religion based on spiritual things rather than physical proof.

The closest that the Bible comes to offering an exact definition is Hebrews 11:1, "Now faith is the assurance of things hoped for, the conviction of things not seen." The Bible also shares in James 2:17 that, "Faith without works is dead." Contributing this to the physical actions of faith, so that one's faith do not die.

Although these definitions are great, both mention things not being in the physical or "not seen." Well, that is not the full story, so with the biblical definition and my own experience as well as others, this is the new definition I have been led by: Faith is the entity of mental, emotional, physical, and spiritual consistent action steps taken prior to a physical phenomenon whether present or beyond the present state.

What ignites and strengthens the fiery faith in us is believing in that faith.

Faith plays as a big umbrella. Belief is under the umbrella of faith that makes it deeper.

It is almost like the umbrella of emotions where they say that anger or fear is the umbrella and under the umbrella are emotions like pain, hurt, disappointment.

Your faith can be challenged and not be able to withstand it, but if you believe in something and have faith in it in your heart, it has a higher chance of withstanding anyone's challenge against it. Mostly because there's an extra zeal that comes with belief and faith combining as a tag team. In most cases, people stand firm on things that have practical proof. Which is why I share these true-life experiences along with what is written. I can share insights for days, months, and years to come and you can probably read this book hundreds of times, but it hits differently when you see the real-life practical experience, the physical proof. Which is why this definition holds true that faith is the entity of mental, emotional, physical, and spiritual consistent action steps taken prior to a physical phenomenon whether present or beyond the present state.

Whether you are a believer or not in *faith*, give yourself the opportunity to simply read through this book. You deserve the chance to know if your experience is truly this third option or if it's not, then at least you know you probably might be actually crazy. Either way, it's a win-win situation to know what is going on with you or someone you know.

So have you been called crazy before?

Normally, people will say being crazy is not a good thing, right? Like there's all the negative connotations attached to the word "crazy."

According to the *Britannica* dictionary, the *Cambridge* dictionary, and the *Oxford* dictionary, these are terms that are used to describe the word "crazy": Not mentally sound: marked by thought or action that lacks reason, being out of the ordinary; *nonsensical*, not sane; unable to think in a clear or sensible way: wild and uncontrolled; *stupid* or not *reasonable*; *mentally ill*, full of cracks or flaws, passionately *preoccupied*.

When viewed logically, because of all of these definitions, most people would not want to be called any of these term names. Yet these terms describe someone who has that fiery faith factor. So if we want to make ourselves feel a bit normal and remove the word "crazy," let's add "fiery" instead. "Fiery," as similar to "crazy," is someone or something that consists of a strong, burning feeling; having a passionate quick temperament at times; and extremely bright nature. Now add "faith" to it, and you have *me*, or maybe *you*, if you've reached this point of this book. So, whether "crazy" or "fiery," as long as "faith" is next to it, it appears to be a bold step.

In the book *Unquenchable*, Carol Kent shines light on some of the fiery things the God of the universe have used fire for. Example, fire has been chosen by God to represent great power, his judgment and wrath, the flaming eyes of the Son of Man upon the throne, his protection, the fiery furnace, his Shekinah glory, the burning bush, the pillar of fire, the burning coal, the flame upon the altar, the chariot of fire, the lake of fire, and the flaming sword guarding Eden.

Let us be honest, to survive in this world, you have to be unapologetically *crazy* (there's good crazy), in our words, "fiery," unapologetically fiery. What makes life even sweeter is being a believer in *Jesus* Christ and the Kingdom of God. You add *faith* to the *crazy*, and life is golden. You move on from the crazy that has a bad connotation to it, to the fiery, one that has a purpose, whether understood or not in the senses. Your fiery, crazy-like faith becomes unapologetically beyond the physical realm and reveals a childlike nature of your true identity. You begin to trust, forgive, and without fear of the known and unknown. Why settle for simplicity and get only the minimum. You can have the cake, eat the whole cake, and receive the golden prize while you're at it.

I know, a terrible analogy, but hopefully, you get the point.

I am unapologetically a believer in the Kingdom of God,, which is why my *faith* is so crazy. But if you pick up this book and you are not Christian, it doesn't mean you cannot relate to what's written in here. You use crazy faith in your life often without even knowing it. You can start utilizing crazy faith today. So do not stop just because you think this is just another religious book. It's not! Plus, this gal is not religious—at all. Let me be the first to agree that the manner in which religion has been used in our world by some people has been divisive. There's a difference between being religious and having a relationship with God (the Almighty God). Anyway, that's a whole other book.

Where was I? Yes, you…me…and this phenomenon we call crazy faith, which we have agreed to call fiery faith, hence the book title.

So how do you decipher from which one of these three options (in denial of your reality, you're just simply crazy, or fiery faith) is running your life?

Let's fact check:
- Track record (God's promises)
  For Believers:
    - What promises has God given you?

- Do you still remember them?
- Do you still believe in them?
- How long has it been? Based on the definition of faith, have you taken the mental, emotional, physical, and spiritual consistent action steps?

Now check God's track record of him doing what he said he would.

For Nonbelievers:
- Who's track record are you fact-checking? Yours? Someone else's?
- Has someone made a promise to you in the past or recently?
- Have you made a promise to yourself recently?

Now fact-check your or that person's track record of doing what you/they said they would?

- Your source

  For Believers:
  - Who or what is your source of faith?
  - Is it honestly still God or yourself or someone else?
  - *Do* you still trust? Do you still believe?
  - Have you been leaning on a resource making it your "source"?

  For Nonbelievers:
  - Who or what is your source ?
  - Do you trust this source wholeheartedly? Has this source ever let you down?
  - Does this source have the ability to fulfill *all* of your needs? Is this source physical?
  - Can this source be defeated or taken away by anyone or anything? Is this source indestructible?
  - Have you been leaning on a resource making it your "source"?

- Efforts toward your belief
  For Believers:
    - Have you taken the mental, emotional, physical, and spiritual consistent action steps?
    - Has patience gotten the best of you?
    - Have pride snuck in during the season of waiting? What made you first begin to have faith?
  For Nonbelievers:
    - What do you believe in?
    - When challenged, can it in any way be defeated by anything or anyone?
    - Are you seeking for more to believe in...?
    - What options are you given yourself?

Supernatural
  For Believers:
  - Is your faith and source consisting of the five senses only or beyond?
  For Nonbelievers:
  - Is your faith and source consisting of the five senses only or beyond?

Fiery Faith Testimony
(as was spoken in 2022)

- My husband and I purchased a home on January 6, 2024.
- I retired from my state job at age thirty-one after five years instead of ten years (September 30, 2024).
- We received enough money to pay off my student loans.

Yep! Retired at thirty-one.
"Possessed the land," huh?
It's time for you to possess the land you are called to.

September 16, 2024
To Whom It May Concern,

    I am writing this letter to express my gratitude to all the staff at the Department of Children and Family Services whom I have had the pleasure of working with. When I initially applied for the job with a master's degree in clinical psychology, I thought it would be just another therapy position, especially since I was working as a Clinician for sex offenders at a prison at the time. However, upon receiving the job offer on the same day at my interview, I became excited about the opportunity to embark on a new career as a Social Worker.

    I am thankful for embracing this new path as it has allowed me to meet wonderful people, overcome new challenges, and create an environment of humility, learning, and love for the past 5 years. However, I have always known that my time with the department was meant to be temporary, and it is with mixed emotions that I announce my departure.

    I will sincerely miss everyone, and I am grateful for all the knowledge and experiences I have gained here. It is amazing to see how God's plan has allowed me to progress in my life and has opened new doors for me—doors beyond my very own imagination.

    With this letter, I officially tender my two weeks' notice. My last day of employment with the Department will be September 30th. I hope this provides enough time for a smooth transition of my caseload.

    As the Department have given me a great experience, I hope in return everyone who has met me in the last 5 years has experienced the love of God, peace, joy, genuineness, laughter, and fond memories. If I have offended anyone during these years without my knowledge, I am sincerely sorry and ask for forgiveness.

I am deeply appreciative of the opportunities and experiences that I have had during the last 5 years. Thank you all so much.

God bless you,
Sincerely,
Rebekah Acquah

True Real-Life Experience

2:00 a.m.
2021

I woke up coughing. Once, a liquid fell down there—again.
Uh-oh, I thought.
I went straight to the bathroom because I already knew what this was…yet a slight hope that it should just be normal discharge. But as I had first thought, that's what it was—blood.
"Not again. I have to pray again to the Lord for this?"
I thought I already prayed for this. But you know, faith works differently.
I sat on the toilet, wiped, and asked my husband to grab my phone. I called the on-call doctor. The lady on the phone asked for my name, phone number, date of birth (which I was okay with), but then she got to the question, "What's the problem?" (or "What's going on?" I can't quite remember her specific words.) I do remember speaking the physical fact of, "I'm bleeding." I said it as low and quick as possible, but then she kept asking questions.
"Are you pregnant?"
Um, now my mind wanted to say, *Obviously. Isn't this ob-gyn on-call answering service?* But I paused and said, "Yes."
Then she asked, "Is it heavy bleeding?"
I honestly was annoyed by now, so I said, trying not to sound like I have an attitude, "I think medium. I don't know heavy."
I guess, not wanting to face what was going on full on, she kept with the questions.

"How far along are you?"

"Look, lady, I don't know. Just get me someone to talk to."

No, I didn't say that, only thought about it.

"I don't know right now. I can't think about it. All I know is that I'm due June 6," I told the lady.

She still wanted the exact number of weeks.

Trying to process my mind to help her while still a bit annoyed, I said. "I know I'm due June 6. I don't know how many weeks that is. Four months maybe? I don't know."

Finally, the questions stopped.

Now I was told to wait to hear back.

Meanwhile, God said, "Have faith. Have faith, my child. I am with you. Grace…will be okay."

Then came my husband. He said, "Let's pray."

He prayed over me and the baby. I believed. I tried to trust again, then I wiped one final time, took a picture as evidence of the blooded tissue, flushed it down, while saying, "The blood of *Jesus* overrides all other blood."

My husband brought me a new pair of underwear. I placed it on, believing it will remain clean.

I told my husband, "Thank you for praying over us (the baby and me). You are Grace's father, and God is the father of us, so I believe and won't say anything else to add to the prayer."

Yet, as I was about to go to sleep, God wasn't done with me.

My husband called me into the office.

"Let me say a word over you."

"Okay," I said.

He held my hand and said, "Since I've known you, one thing that I've always seen and know of is *your faith*, your faith in GOD and your belief in your scripture, *Jeremiah 29:11*. So have faith, trust God. Grace is okay. Pray and talk to God."

He said much more, but those few words at the beginning were all I needed. God was speaking. I thanked my husband and thanked GOD in my heart for speaking to me through him. I grabbed my Bible as I went back to the bedroom, opened up Jeremiah 29:11, and did what I was instructed to do, believing that was God telling me through my husband: how to seal it and get some rest. I *prayed, "Thank you, God,"* then *assured him that I trusted him* and *love him*. And I smiled!

You see crazy faith works like that. You believe first, and then God *uses* that to water the first belief, which becomes a faith where you can go to sleep laughing and smiling with the words "Thank you, Jesus, I trust you," and have faith…crazy faith.

It was almost an hour, and the on-call doctor did not call. Oh, but my Doctor God has already sealed it all with his blood; so I put on Spirit-filled worship and, with a big smile, went to sleep.

While I was asleep, the doctor called about an hour later. I had already decided to continue with my faith in God, but I listened as she suggested that I get an ultrasound in the morning to reassure that all is okay. I agreed.

The next morning, I was called in for a nine-thirty appointment. I went in not knowing what I should expect. You see faith is not something one can see, but it's something one believes in and do. But suddenly, as I waited thirty minutes for the ultrasound to begin, I cried. I sent my pastor a message to pray for me and my baby. I drank two cups of water and kept the faith. How? Well, as I saw all of the pregnant women around with big, medium, and small bellies, I thought, *Wow, and here I am in between believing if the child I'm carrying is still alive or not.*

How crazy faith works is. Although you're the one in the room going through the emotions, you can still recognize the beauty of life around and still be grateful. So I remember the words of my pastor and kept repeating them: "It is well with you and your child." So no matter the results of the ultrasound, "It is well with you and your child."

Ultrasound time.

"Rebekah."

"Yes, I'm here," I answered.

I went into the room and was told it would be a topical ultrasound. She attempted the topical. As she pressed on my belly, I felt a sudden rush of liquid, and I figured that must be blood, and surely, it was. Then she asked for an internal ultrasound, which I knew would have been the case. I wiped and then began the internal ultrasound.

At this point, I felt immune to whatever the results would be, so I asked, "Is the baby still there?"

She said, "Yes, *but…*"

Uh-oh, get ready for it, Rebekah.
"But there's no heartbeat."
What should I do now? I thought. *Cry or what?*

No, as hard as it was, I left the ultrasound room thanking Jesus, not in disbelief as one would think, just grateful that God chose me to use for a miracle or to have a story to help someone along the line of this life. Woah, crazy, right? I thought another blessing that I can help someone through.

So I said almost immediately, "Lord, I believe that your grace is sufficient."

Next, I met with the midwife at 11:00 a.m., on November 15, 2021, who confirmed that the baby doesn't have a heartbeat and that there hasn't been any growth since the last ultrasound. She went on to name the options I had. Option one, wait it out for the baby to bleed out like a normal menstrual period; option two, use a prescription to help take the baby out; option three, have surgery to remove the baby. Well, that *crazy faith* mentality said option one. I calmly said I will wait. In hopes that, yes, this was indeed a miracle story. So I left in laughter and joy, a little confused in the back of my head. But crazy faith is believing even when physically all else says otherwise.

December 15, 2021—I lost the child.

December 16, 2021—It wasn't over. Huge sac came out looking like blood and little particles.

December 16, 2021—Quiet time with God. Relief and from the burden of being hopeful. A time of mourning and tears, physically allowing myself to cry and have a conversation with God.

The thing about crazy faith is not that denial is prevalent; it is more so leaning toward accepting reality but yet being hopeful for the things not yet seen to be one day seen in the physical. Some may say this takes strength. I beg the differ, because, for me, it was not about "being strong." Losing a child, especially one who you've named, and then going through the prolonged process of waiting for that child to come out of you dead, is a tough thing to go through. So strength is not enough for situations like this. I believe that all things work together for those who trust and believe in the plans of the Lord, and that is what took me through: belief and faith in the words of the Source.

Chapter

2

Words

If any of you lack wisdom, let him ask of God, that giveth to all men liberally, and upbraideth not; and it shall be given him. But let him ask in faith, nothing wavering. For he that wavereth is like a wave of the sea driven with the wind and tossed. (James 1:5–6 KJV)

Romans 10:8 talks about believing with your heart (first) and then confessing with your mouth. Even the world's best-selling book (the Bible) knows that words are important, yet the belief comes from the heart, then faith is established. All right, let's say you're not a believer in this world-renowned book called the Bible. Well, actions do speak louder as some will say. Let's go to this real-life experience.

True Real-Life Experience

"Be careful, you shouldn't be going to that place by yourself. You never know what could happen. You're too young to be going and be with homeless people all by yourself, spending hours getting too close.

My response, "No worries, I hear you, but I have *faith* God is with me. He placed this on my heart, so I must go."

Rebekah Acquah

The Outcome

I went and was blessed to hear many stories of the homeless lifestyle. I gained relationships and was kept safe the entire time. I then experienced sleeping in my car for two weeks due to my circumstances at the time.

Ministry in Newark Penn Station changed my perspective on what it meant to have faith. From as young as I can remember, there was always a connection between me and those who did not have much. Here is a journal entry on my outreach to the homeless in Newark Penn Station.

> Today was a very good day. It was more than good; it was a blessing. Today was the first day of the beginning of my goal and dream of helping the homeless and being there for them, even if it's just to give an ear to their stories about life, or maybe to give some change here and there, or even to give them snacks or something to eat. I know I can't do much right now, but just putting a smile on someone's face makes me happy. What God has taught me in life is to give, even if it's your last. Well, if you feel it's your last, because you are a child of God, it's never your last. You have a Father who provides what you need and protect you even if you don't notice His protection. He loves you when you feel there's no more love in this world. Today marked my first visit to Newark Penn Station. I visited my third family (others call them the homeless). They are my family because they give me hope. They make me feel more appreciated, and they help my trust to grow, because they trust strangers for so many years to donate to them, no matter how many rejections and negativity they've experienced. If a person can still get up and continue to ask those same people for help and money every day of their life for years, I see that as courage. My third family has courage and faith. I met Jackie,

Elliot, Vance, and a few others; but I remember Elliot and Jackie most because I actually conversed with them. Our conversation was the most pleasurable, special and blessed moment of my day. Jackie is a fifty-year-old married woman who lost her legs. Now I met her sitting in her wheelchair under a metal roof/covering. It was so cold outside today, but she was all bundled up, which made me happy inside that at least she was warm. Our conversation automatically started, and if I'm not mistaken, it lasted for about twenty to thirty minutes. Jackie told me she was homeless for nine years, since 2005, the year she lost her legs. And guess what? Her son died because he was shot in a drive-by shooting. He saved two people and didn't even know he got shot until he was suffering from internal bleeding and died (tears). Jackie never went to college, but she has two daughters: one graduated with a bachelor's degree, and the other went to college but only stayed three to four days and dropped out because she did not think college was for her. Jackie has family members as well. Now some people may ask why was she homeless for nine years, and honestly, I asked Jackie the same question. When she told me that she and her husband had been married for twenty-nine years, I thought that was a very wonderful thing. I said to her, "Wow, that's wonderful and a blessing that you've been married that long, but I'm curious. Please if I may ask, why you are homeless then?" She said, "At the time, we weren't divorced, but we were separated, and my daughter couldn't take care of me because she was in college." She then pointed across the street showing me where she used to sleep. She explained how she would sit all day outside by a pole, which she showed me. I learned a lot about Jackie, and I was very interested in her life story. It seemed as though all she wanted was to talk to somebody. As our conversation continued, tears rested in my eyes.

I tried to turn my face a bit so that Jackie wouldn't see the tears. I learned that almost everyone died in threes, from Jackie's friends to her family members. She found her brother dead at home on the floor due to brain damage from alcohol. Her mother and father passed away as well. Then I asked her how she lost her legs. My curiosity and concern led to a very sad truth after she said these words: "From being homeless for so long, in these streets, my legs was no good anymore." She continued, "This is what people don't understand, do you think I want to have no legs? I didn't want to be homeless, but they don't realize what we go through, and until a person becomes homeless and experiences what we experience, it will be hard for them to know the struggle and truth. I thank God because I know it wasn't my time to go. That's why even though I was homeless for nine years, I am still alive today, and things are getting better. They're not all good yet, but I am blessed because I have an apartment now, and I'm not homeless anymore." Jackie was absolutely right, and that is exactly what I told her. She was even concerned about me, whether she was holding me up from going somewhere or not. Not knowing that she was the reason why I was there, I simply told her, "No, I'm okay. I love talking to you, and you're not holding me up." She asked me where I came from, and I told her I live on campus at a university. This is when her daughters came up in the conversation. Her oldest daughter is twenty-four years old, so by doing the math, I realized that her daughter was fifteen when Jackie became homeless and lost her son. During our conversation, people walked by. Some stared at me like I was crazy, and a few stopped and gave Jackie a dollar in her cup. Avery, a generous man even gave her $13. God bless his soul.

A young female passing by stopped to ask Jackie, "If anybody could help you with one thing what would you want?" Jackie replied, "My legs." The young lady was shocked and said to Jackie, "I can't give you your legs, but what else would you want?" Jackie paused and said, "Nothing then, because I have an apartment now." I then jumped in and said she was homeless for nine years. This fact shocked the young lady again, and she simply said, "Wow, nine years." Her friend was waiting for her, so she told Jackie, "I'll talk to you again, hopefully." Jackie replied, "You'll see me here again at this same spot tomorrow." Their brief two-minute conversation just affirmed to me what I always thought about my third family (homeless people). They are human beings just like us and are not selfish or greedy. They do not want all your money or want to be on drugs. They are just like you and me; and even better because, like Jackie, they have hearts; and all they want is one thing: their life back. It could be their family back, their home back, their job back that they lost because of the economy, their honor back, and, as in Jackie's case, their legs back. Jackie was very honest throughout our conversation. I could tell it was all honesty. She kept bringing up God and faith and blessings, and even if she made the simplest mistake where she didn't recall a situation in her life correctly, she said, "Sorry, Lord," and corrected herself. After the conversation with the young lady while I was thinking how wonderful this woman Jackie was, a man came to Jackie and gave her a pack of cigarettes (which wasn't filled). I must admit it was very cold outside, and I was freezing a bit, so that made me ask Jackie, "How long is the person you're waiting for going to be before they come?" She told me that was her husband. He's the one that was waiting for her, and he's very protective of her and shy. I waved to him. I still was thinking why they were in this cold if they had an apartment. Now that I think about it, being homeless for nine years at the same spot day to day month and years going by, a person will certainly find it hard to not come back to that same spot after gaining a home. Perhaps Jackie has gotten so used to being homeless and sitting in that spot that every day, she felt that's where her true home is. Perhaps that became more of a home than a building, so it will take time to stop coming back or getting used to not being homeless. She told me how she still reminisces on her son's death and still misses him. Of course, a mother will never forget her child, especially by the manner in which she lost her baby boy. I reassured Jackie to stay warm, and I hoped that she would be leaving soon. Then she asked for my number, and we exchanged phone numbers, in hopes that maybe when I call her, it would be the call that would make her day better. She tried to give me a handshake, but I simply gave her a hug. She said it was nice talking to me and that was what she needed. She thought I was a sweet girl, and hopefully, I would call her. We said our goodbyes, and I was off on my way back inside of Newark Penn Train Station. This is where I met my next family member, Elliot, who introduced me to his brother Vance. Walking into Newark Station, there weren't many people earlier, but then I guess around that time (not knowing exactly how long I've been at the station) there were more people (family, homeless) than before, so I looked for a spot to sit and someone to talk to. My goal was to talk to and connect with women, so I sat next to a family (homeless) woman and said, "Hi." She didn't really respond much, even when I asked for her name. But her expression looked like she was one of my family members who suffered from mental illness. On my right, there was a man standing up eating ramen noodles (the cup looked like it had been kept for days, or even weeks), but his look brought peace because he was happy and enjoyed his meal. I said hi and he replied hi. That's how I met Elliot.

We began our conversation. Elliot is a fifty-four-year-old man (which I never would've guessed because he looked ten years younger) who had two brothers. He was the middle child. He lived in Newark and went to an institute and graduated. He comes to Newark Penn every day and has an eighty-year-old mother who is a registered nurse (RN). He said she comes to the station to help the homeless at times. I told Elliot about my school, and he asked me what was I studying. I told him clinical psychology, which he figured that I liked people, and I affirmed that to him. We even started talking about each other's families, and he asked about my parents. That's when he found out that I was African, and that's when I found out he was good at math because he guessed the age I came to America based on what I told him. Elliot is a very nice man, and during our conversation, his brother came, and I was introduced to Vance, who made me laugh. He said, "My name is Vance, as in *dance, lance,* …" It was funny how he said it. It reminds me of how Jackie made me laugh when she was telling the story about her legs and the man who gave her a very tall prosthetic leg and it made her taller than every man, so she had to take it off to feel better. Vance was also nice, and I felt comfortable with both of them. I don't understand why people are scared to talk to people who are homeless if they've never made an attempt to hurt them. They are homeless, but they are people. Elliot asked me if I could spare two dollars, and I told him the truth on why I couldn't grant his request. He did not stop talking to me nor did he get upset; he simply said, "Okay, I understand. God bless you for even talking to me." He asked me if I come to the station every week, and I explained to him I used to stop there on my way home, but I'd stopped, and I had just started again. I planned to return every Wednesday though. He seemed happy to hear that news. I was so into the conversation that I almost forgot that I had a train to catch. I quickly looked at the time and told Elliot I had to go but would return next week. He shook my hand and said, "See you next week, and keep warm."

I told him to keep warm tonight as well and said goodbye to him and his brother Vance.

They now know me as Gloria-Rebekah.

So, yes, I had a *wonderful, happy,* and *very blessed day* on February 12, 2013. I learned a lot and I appreciated a lot as well. Today is the first day for a lifetime of memories with my third family, aka the homeless. I can't wait for next week. God bless the homeless. God gives, let's give. "God Gives, let's Give" is a phrase that has been revealed to me through a dream to help God's people, those in need of a friend, a sister or a helper, and those in poverty. Today I understood the reasons behind my experiences so far.

I later went through more experiences with the homeless. Not only through speaking with them but through my own personal homelessness for two weeks. I had been taking summer classes for two years without an issue with the university, paying for my room and board during the summer. But this summer, 2014, was different. Room and board was no longer covered during the summer due to funding being cut, and there was no way I was going to not take my free summer classes that will enable me to graduate on time or even early. I knew I couldn't travel every day for an hour on the train to class. I would've been late, plus the expense on my aunt to ask her for money when I didn't have all the time, even though she wouldn't have minded. I still believed there was another way. I began the summer by asking my friend, who was a residential assistant to sleep over, but there's a limited amount of time that visitors are allow to sleep over. I slept in my car for the remaining weeks of my summer classes. I did not mention anything to anyone, not even my aunt. My routine for the two and a half weeks was to wake up at 5:00 a.m. when it's a bit dark; change into my clothes for the day; use a bottle of water and the travel-size toothpaste I got from CVS store; and brush my teeth. Then without showering, I put deodorant on, wash my face, and wait for sunlight to come out to head to the library as I waited for class. After class, I would either meet up with my friend, hang out, eat something, and tell her I would see her tomorrow. When she asked if I was going home, I answered, "Something like that." I would head to my car or to the library to charge my phone to 100 percent because they closed late. In my car, I would have my phone in hand while I prayed with the gospel music on, and head to the back seat to sleep soundly. I got used to the routine, and fear was far away from me. I still made my trips to visit my homeless family at Newark Penn. I felt protected and covered by the hands of God every day in my car. After classes ended, I returned home and received an A for the summer. That summer I gained so much appreciation and love for those who have no home or a place to go for education. I didn't know that my experience for the two and a half weeks was to understand my purpose that God would later reveal to me in fullness in my life.

True Real-Life Experience No .2

"You have to apply to schools you know you will get accepted to. That school you're thinking about applying to, it's so hard to get in with the grades you have, plus they only accept fourteen students a year. The program is tough. It's also two weeks before the deadline, they probably already chose who they are accepting."

My response, "Well, I'll still apply because I know I'll get in. I believe God has high standards for me, so I have *faith*. I cannot be scared.

The Outcome

I was accepted into the program right away. The only African/African American in the program, to everyone's surprise. I also became the commencement speaker for all the graduate school graduating class. In a time where faith is not honored to be placed into speeches meant for the public, I could not have done this speech without this amazing phenomenon and my lifestyle in fiery faith. So, yes, you guessed it right.

When I created my speech, I was told that I had to shorten it, which is understood, and then I was asked if I must include the faith piece in it.

"Most definitely."

Here is the final copy of my speech as commencement speaker for a program I was told not to apply to and that I was surely the weakest link in the program. A program I got dismissed from but never stopped attending even after my dismissal.

UMass Dartmouth Graduate School
Graduation Speech
(2018-2019)

To the Chancellor, Distinguished guests, Professors, Students, Parents, family, friends and most importantly my fellow graduates: good afternoon and welcome to the UMass, Dartmouth Graduate School Graduation Ceremony of the Class of 2019. Wow! We've waited years to hear this sentence. I am sure we are all grateful to be here today as this day sets the stage of a great accomplishment, and many more to come. We definitely wouldn't have made it this far without our support systems, our family, and friends. Can we please stand and give them a hand. Graduates today is probably the majority of us last days on the soils of Umass Dartmouth. As we depart I hope we keep this formula in mind (Second chances + Faith + hard work + perseverance = Success). With these four things, we can do anything! They are true formulas for success and I would like to show you how.

First I thank God for trusting me to stand before you today. Trust me when I say my being here is truly a miracle. So, let's talk about second chances, Umass Dartmouth is known for second chances. Think on your life, when were you given another chance to turn a negative into positive. How did you get here, we know it wasn't alone. I for one did not get here alone.

A refugee from west Africa Liberia, born during a 14 years civil war that led to over 200,000 deaths, Where my mother would sacrifice herself to feed me as she stayed hungry for days. Leaving my country in tears at age 8 with a loving single teenage mother behind, it would be another 16 years before I would see her again. At the time this 8 year old girl was told that she was coming to America, a place she never heard of; A place where at a young age her second war began. She experience,Depression, physical abuse, mental abuse, sexual abuse, sleeping in a car, suicidal thoughts and attempts, sleepless nights and many fights with herself and others; she was told she will never be something in life, threaten to be sent back to Africa; and ironically at this very moment today, she was supposed to be in Liberia pregnant and uneducated. She stand before you today only because she received a second chance, one that was given by God in a disguise of her aunt Miss Evelyn Williams, a woman who was also refused an education. Took her in and made it known to this now teenager the importance of an EDUCATION. No matter what surrounded her receiving an education was the only constant thing she knew.

Graduates, I reminisce on this girl's story as a reminder of how connected we all are. As I have listened to my classmates who also have similar life journeys. Like Ashley Estacio who manages three jobs, owning a home, taking care of family, dealing with several medical conditions and still was able to maintain a 4.0 GPA in Graduate school. I stand here not just for myself, but I stand here representing, all of us, the graduates and our families. All those who have struggled, all those who wanted to give up, all those who imagined receiving a degree but life got in the way somehow, those who have quit before and don't know how to start over again, those who have been dismissed from programs yet recovered, those who take care of loved ones yet go unseen, and anyone who may have even been depressed or homeless at some point. Graduates we all represent each other, today we are all now a part of the University of Massachusetts-Dartmouth family. We gave ourselves second chances!

We also represent the parents, significant others and best friends who hear our tireless cries about how difficult graduate school has been. Thank you families, we greatly appreciate you! We represent professors who have multiple jobs, yet still manage to attend classes and teach with their all. Thank you, Dr. Ted Powers, the clinical program director. We represent the financial aid department who help students stay in school and graduate (thank you Ms. Korrine Peterson!). We represent the conduct and dispute panel who gave us second chances. Thank you, Mary Beckwith. Lastly, we represent everyone else in the audience who needs representation in order to give you hope of believing once more that you deserve a second chance. We represent you. Now let's talk about FAITH, HARD WORK, and PERSEVERANCE, where the formula continues, three things prominent in the course of our years here at Umass Dartmouth. It helped me believe again, and you've use these three without knowing it.

Graduates, one thing we have assurance of now are that we are MASTERS and DOCTORS in our various fields, and with these titles comes Masters and Doctoral problems. There's a saying "more money more problems", but in our case, "more degrees more problems to solve". Nonetheless, we are confident, because UMASS Dartmouth has prepared us for the journey ahead. With the outstanding preparation given along with FAITH, HARD WORK, AND PERSEVERANCE, we are destined for success.

FAITH. Faith in God and faith in ourselves. Many of us have faith. Some may call it hope, chance or coincidence. Throughout our years at UMass Dartmouth there were times when the odds were stacked against us, with so many applicants and limited spots, we all were chosen to be here and our faith kept us here. I was told I couldn't make it, yet here I am. As a refugee from Liberia, raised by a single aunt, I've been through everything that should've left me broken or dead, many of us may not have had the highest GPAs, or greatest personal statement that shined light on our passion to make a difference, meanwhile we had these items in the formula of success and was accepted into the programs of our dreams. I mean, come on, that had to count for something, right? (laughter). Success simply doesn't manifest with faith alone. We were accepted, but the hard work had to follow.

Enter HARD WORK: What we do prior and after will keep that thing we hoped for going. As my Professor Dr. Joshua Masse would describe this as "The ABC's of a behavior." Sometimes, I get it, we put in the hard work and what we expected doesn't happen. At least not right away. Many people say hard work gets you places I say, it's not that simple. This is why these three things work together; one cannot work without the other. When the hard work is engaged, perseverance the persistence in us graduating despite how difficult or the delays we faced in achieving success. When faith is activated the hard work and perseverance must follow, when perseverance stands, faith and hard work contributes to complete the trio. Without these three I wouldn't be standing here before you.

When I had my three panic attacks at the very beginning of my program, faith and perseverance was there to pick me up. When I was dismissed from my program, due to having a 2.5 GPA a little below the program requirement. Working two jobs, 80–120 hours a week and grad school, my fellow grads we all can relate, this was most of us "the struggle was real." Faith and perseverance couldn't do it alone, Faith kept us in, yet hard work towards staying in the program had to be activated. The opportunities we've received here at Umass Dartmouth will change our lives forever. Just as my Aunty Evelyn gave me a second chance, think about who has given you second chances or how you gave yourself a second chance by applying to your program. Umass Dartmouth is known for giving second chances. When I received the dismissal letter, the first thing I did was smile, yes, I said "I smile" and then I started dancing with joy…no, I wasn't losing my mind trust me…I wasn't crazy either. What I was, was hopeful or as I would call it faithful. I became immediately happy at the sight of that dismissal letter because I saw a challenge, I didn't see dismissal, didn't feel rejected, did not think it was the end, I saw my FAITH manifesting in the HARD WORK that I was about to put in and PERSEVERE if given another opportunity (SECOND CHANCE). Umass Dartmouth, gave me another opportunity, seeing the opportunity to rise above what looked like defeat. I PERSEVERED. GRADUATES WE PERSEVERED.

We have everything we need academically to fulfill our dreams forward and achieve goals we seek out to achieve. Just in case you find challenging times, and when those Masters and Doctoral problems become overwhelming, see in the moment what is actually not in front of you…see success. Give yourself a Chance, Have Faith, put in the Hard Work and Persevere.

Remember the formula (S+F+H+P =Success!)

Congratulations, Class of 2019

* * * *

How many times have you been told no and still went after that thing? How many times have you been challenged by others that you couldn't do something amazing, but you continue anyway.

It's not solely about the outcome, more so was about the mindset, actions, and fiery *faith*: You were partaking in that act of faith.

There's a point of faith that makes it crazy. So, what makes it crazy or fiery?

Looking beyond the senses. Looking beyond the voices of others who sometimes may mean well, yet if they are giving advice that only confirms information about the five senses (touch, seeing, hearing, taste, sight) they are limiting your fire. Looking beyond our own shortcomings. Looking beyond our background and pressing on no matter what. Yet as stated in chapter 1, this fiery-ness works best if what you believe in comes from a supernatural source that cannot be taken away from you, or else we may be setting ourselves up for disappointment, because remember we must look beyond the five senses.

There was a chosen vessel called Fred Price who taught on faith, and a few things I heard was that "the just shall live by faith," so if we are breathing, we must be living, and we live and breathe 24/7, right? Therefore, faith should be practiced and lived 24/7 if you deemed yourself to be among the "just." What makes your everyday faith fiery is that if it is an everyday thing. Every time it is tested (which most would say during difficult times or out of what we deemed as hard and difficult situation), we are given an option, either to stop believing, hide, give up on life; or the option to remain positive, calm, and fervent in the good things that we believe our source has given us, both in the present and to come. The fiery part is in the latter. It is okay for your faith to be tested by fire, hence, becoming fiery.

> For no one can lay a foundation other than that which is laid, which is Jesus Christ. Now if anyone builds on the foundation with gold, silver, precious stones, wood, hay, straw—each one's work will become manifest, for the Day will disclose it, because it will be revealed by fire, and the fire will test what sort of work each one has done. If the work that anyone has built

on the foundation survives, he will receive a reward. If anyone's work is burned up, he will suffer loss, though he himself will be saved, but only as through fire. (1 Corinthians 3:11–15)

Faith Exercise

List one thing you are believing in God, your source, to do in your life.

Name the obstacles that have the potential to block this from happening (highest possibility to lowest):

Mental	Emotional	Physical	Spiritual

1.
2.
3.
4.
5.
6.
7.

List a second thing you are believing in God, your source, to do in your life.

Name the obstacles that have the potential to block this from happening (highest possibility to lowest):

Mental	Emotional	Physical	Spiritual

1.
2.
3.
4.
5.
6.
7.

Fiery FAITH

List the third thing you are believing in God, your source, to do in your life.

Name the obstacles that have the potential to block this from happening (highest possibility to lowest):

    Mental   Emotional   Physical   Spiritual

1.
2.
3.
4.
5.
6.
7.

Writing these down gives you the opportunity of awareness. Although there may be some surprises we may encounter, yet be aware that even when they come, you are intentional of overcoming. My hope for you is that you will not need to come back to this list to cross out anything because we want to also practice fiery faith in a positive light of believing that negative things may not need to happen to have what has been promised to you. It is important to not plant a self-defeating seed alongside your faith seed; therefore, utilize this list you created as a reference of the action steps of physically removing them from your mind, then writing it on paper so that will remain exactly there where it belongs, on paper, away from your mind, which represents a space that whatever is there has a higher possibility of producing fruits. We want whatever is in your mind to produce good fruits.

> If you remain in me and my words remain in you, ask whatever you wish, and it will be done for you. This is to my Father's glory, that you bear much fruit, showing yourselves to be my disciples. (John 15:7–8 NIV)

If you remain or abide in Him, he knows you will never ask for things that go against his word. You're not going to ask for something stupid.

God has laid the foundation by giving us a faith seed. You must build on this faith seed. Even so faith, if it hath not works, is dead, being alone. Faith needs proof as well in the works.

Therefore, it is not wise to contribute faith to lack of having facts, because the facts are in the works. For most people who identify with faith, the facts are in their personal past experiences that they have struggled through the burning of the fire successfully, that the works have shown and igniting and growing their faith even more. Faith is ongoing.

God wants you to have your desires. If He didn't, He would just program us. He would have you like the animals. (Have you seen a squirrel when a car is coming? For some reason, it runs toward the car rather than away from the car, most likely killing itself in the end.)

You have the priceless gift of choice.

God's word tries to influence your choice to protect you, not control your choice.

Your word must match your actions steps of what you have proclaimed in a heartfelt belief. Test the words of others if they do not match what the true source words have stated concerning your situation.

So, if you know the words, especially the words for your life of the source you believe and have faith in (assuming your source is good), when others attempt to place words against things happening in your life favorably, whose words will you believe?

Chapter

3

All Seasons

2006

"You are useless and will amount to nothing."

March 2020

"Do you take Rebekah to be your wife?"
"I do."

December 2021

Twelve weeks ultrasound:
"I'm sorry, but there's no heartbeat, and it looks like the baby is measuring at only eleven weeks. Do you want to remove it surgically, by taking medication, or allow it to discharge naturally from your body?"

October 2022

"Congratulations, it's a handsome baby boy."

January 2024

"The adoption of your child is going through."

Crazy faith is meant to occur in all seasons: the good seasons and the wintering storms in your life. Having a crazy faith does not mean you are exempt from the highs and lows of life. It rather helps you through them. There will be moments of walking through frightening, death-like valley (Psalm 23:4).

It's the seasons of life that you go through that makes *faith* crazier. The consistency of your faith is what allows it the privilege of being *crazy* or, in our case, fiery. Which leads us to the great phenomenon of the grace to be patient.

*****

Water and fire are very powerful illustrations of sources that cannot be easily understood. The God of the heavens uses both water and fire to describe who He is: "I am the living water," "holy ghost fire."

Just as the fire that ignites in a forest does not just burn up the entire forest at once, for each tree in the forest takes time before it becomes ashes. While there may be fire on the east, it takes time before the fire reaches the west. The same as a stream of water, the waves begin at one end and take time after it touches anything in its way, before reaching the end of the stream line.

It takes *patience*. Patience will reveal the will of God to you.

> For ye have need of patience, that, after ye have done the will of God, ye might receive the promise. (Hebrews 10:36)

There's an older man's true story in the best-selling book, the Bible. To be exact, he was one hundred years old, and his wife was ninety. Their names were Abraham and Sarah, and they were obviously over the ages of having children. As the woman yearned to have a child; so their source, the God and Creator of the heavens, promised them a child, which seemed impossible at their age. After twenty years of waiting, of course, it was easy to forget the promise. But God didn't forget. This is seen in Hebrews 6:15. After Abraham had patiently endured, he obtained the promise that his source, who is the God and Creator of the heavens, promised him. Sarah became pregnant with a baby boy, Isaac, who brought them laughter and joy in their old age.

There's a season of silence from God, our source in moments of faith, but the fire continues to burn. In this season, we should be mindful of others giving their opinions on us as we await for what we believe would happen.

Once it begins with God, the source, we must remain steadfast in what was said. This is why it is important for the faith to start fiery, so the fire can burn until the promise comes to fruition. Stay, even when it does not make sense. Let that fire burn away the doubts and voices of naysayers.

That "crazy" that people keep calling you, claim it and fight for it to remain. Do not try to be normal in the patience of faith. We have the opportunity during the waiting season to spend the waiting period knowing and studying our source more and identifying ourselves and purpose in the source. We are not simple creations; there are so many aspects and dimensions of who we are.

I have toddlers, and I've come to realize that we begin our journey of this tiny seed of faith as children, as young as an infant. These gifts of free-spirited souls come into the world without any idea of all these strangers around them are. Yet they have no other options but to trust that they are safe and will be love and cared for. So they smile, even moments after being told no. They may make many mistakes yet still continue to walk by faith, believing that their "strangers" will not throw them away or give up on them. Some children who receive punishments after making terrible mistakes will still innocently go with a hug and comfort to the very person that they received the spanking from. In my experience as a therapist and a child protection social worker, I have seen many times children who were abused and yet some of these abused children would still want to live with their parents.

Some will say, "That's crazy," which is the point exactly. Children innocently are crazy little faith seeds walking about, and they trust, even in fear at times, although some of these situations are dangerous and not all parents present themselves to be good parents in their actions. Imagine having a source whose characteristics are only meant for good.

Imagine trusting such a source like one of the innocent children's trust. No matter the circumstance, the punishments in life, the good and the bad, we still run back to this all-knowing, good, and perfect Source, trusting that this Source wants the very best for us and is here to care for us, despite us not knowing everything about this Source.

Like a toddler, we can relate to the God of the heavens and Creator of the earth as Father, trusting that we are and will be well cared for. My toddler's YouTube kids show *Bible Adventure* gave an example of a bug name Blinky who was given bubbles to play with by an older rock named Mr. Stone. Blinky was instructed by Mr. Stone to share the bubbles with his friends; and if the bubbles finish, since he is sharing with his friends, Mr. Stone promises he will give Blinky more bubbles. So Blinky's friends came to play with the bubbles, but suddenly, Blinky became afraid that if he shares his bubbles it will run out. He told his star friend that he does not want the bubble to run out. His star friend then asked him, "What did Mr. Stone say about the bubbles?" He was trying to remind him what Mr. Stone said. Blinky told the exact words of Mr. Stone to him regarding sharing the bubbles and not worrying about it being finished. His star friend then asked him why doesn't he "obey and trust" the words of Mr. Stone. Blinky then was led to pray to God to help him obey and trust Mr. Stone's word and promise to him. Blinky began to share the bubbles with his friends and, in turn, had an amazing fun experience with his friends. He forgot whether or not it would run out as he trusted in obedience. Blinky was taught that we show faith every day when we trust and obey.

As my toddler show says, "I show faith every day when I trust and obey."

Faith is an intentional everyday decision. In every season, trust. Show obedience to the promise and allow our action steps to live what we believe. So let's share our bubble with a friend and trust our Mr. Stone will provide and supply all good things that we need to sustain us in this life and beyond.

Faith Exercise

List three things you've been waiting on/for.
1.
2.
3.

List three struggles you've had while waiting? (Emotional, physical, mental, spiritual)
1.
2.
3.

Name three things you can begin to do today that will bring you back to trusting the original word and promise:
1. The emotional step I can take is _____
2. Physical practical steps I can take is _____
3. Spiritual step I can take is _____

True Real-Life Experience

I was led by God to write my first book, *Unquenchable: The Burning Bush Within*, in 2017. Success of this book did not manifest until 2023, six years later. Now this book you are reading is my third.

How long can your fire burn in the waiting season?

Who's the source of your fiery faith?

Chapter

4

Obedience

Obedience to Move in Action

Faith without works is *dead*. (James 2:26.)

But someone will say, "You have faith, and I have works." Show me your faith apart from your works, and I will show you my faith by my works. (James 2:18)

God will not give you what he knows you will mismanage. Your works have to show and be tested that you will be obedient with what may be given to you. You have to prepare for an even more increased act of faith.

A question we must ask ourselves is, are we willing to grow in wisdom, in discernment, and in our spirituality as spirit being in a human body operating on earth? Are we knowledgeable enough to understand that nothing is really what meets the natural eyes, so that when your "intuition" is saying otherwise, will we be brave enough to heed obedience?

There is something in you, in the way you process things that makes you unique. One person may see someone or a situation as obnoxious, yet you see that same situation or person as expressive, expressive in themselves, seeing beyond what is physically in front. Faith becomes fiery only after we connect with our spirit man. Once our spirit man takes over—assuming we have gone through the process of identifying with a good source, that is—obedience to our spirit man becomes highly important in thriving in a fiery faith mindset. The greatest source is the Holy Spirit, as we are spirit beings. Because the outside world cannot see with the common eye, you connect with your spirit man. We call ourselves humans (hu – meaning embodiment of God, Man- the species). God is in us all as a species on this Earth. It takes another person having a deeper level of spirituality to be able to understand why you are being obedient and have changed to take actions steps in different areas of your life.

Some may say, "You've change" or "You're not the same anymore" or "Um, can I have the old you back, this other you is weird" or "Who do you think you are now, chill out" or "Ohh-kay, Ms./Mr. Spirit Person, no one cares, you're going a bit overboard crazy" or "Let's leave God out of this" and more.

It is very difficult to obey anything, so having to obey something or someone that no one else can physically see with their eyes, one that lives inside of you, and you have to try to explain to people at a level they can understand, yeah, that can be difficult and a huge struggle. Yet obedience takes action steps in order for the practice of fiery faith to be manifested in the physical. Remembering the definition, we said faith is: faith is the entity of mental, emotional, physical, and spiritual consistent action steps taken prior to a physical phenomenon whether present or beyond the present state.

Eventually, the works of those action steps will produce its fruits for physical eyes to see.

True Real-Life Experience

First, we must have a strong conviction of believing in the word that was given to us prior to taking action steps. The conviction must be an immovable one.

> Therefore, my beloved brothers are steadfast, immovable, always abounding in the work of the Lord

knowing that in the Lord your labor is not in vain. (1 Corinthians 15:58)

Imagine going on a trip that everyone is against, but you have been convicted to go on this trip. You have no idea what is there, but you just know strongly you must go and all you hear is "I am with you. Do not fear. Go."

Action steps:
- Mental action steps can be seen in thanksgiving to the Source for using you as a vessel to answer yours and others prayers.
- Physical action steps will be by preparing all the necessary things needed for the trip, and physically ensuring safety as much as you can physically without stressing yourself out about the outcome.
- Spiritual action steps may be praying over the trip or connecting to the Source, asking for deeper clarity if it's possible. Overall, obedience is completing this faith task to the finest and going on the trip with an openness as you have been convicted to "go."

With faith, sometimes the answer may come immediately, as long as you are in consistent contact with the source of your faith. On the other hand, it may not be an immediate answer.

> And he came and took her by the hand, and lifted her up; and immediately the fever left her, and she ministered unto them. (Mark 1:31)

> And immediately Jesus stretched forth [his] hand, and caught him, and said unto him, O thou of little faith, wherefore didst thou doubt? (Mathew 14:31)

> And the Lord visited Sarah as he had said, and the Lord did unto Sarah as he had spoken. For Sarah conceived, and bare Abraham a son in his old age, at the set time of which God had spoken to him. (Jonah 1:17)

> After being in the belly of the great fish for three days and nights, Jonah prayed to the Lord, and then God

commanded the fish to vomit Jonah onto dry land. (Jonah 2:10)

Faith Exercise

List three things that you have been praying for and believing to happen. Remember these three things *you must* not have doubt be hesitant to write them. You must believe that the Source is fully capable to bring these three to fruition.

You are writing these things because
- writing makes it permanent and
- writing allows you to take it out of your head/heart

and see it in front of you coming to life. This allows the next ideas or thoughts to now have room to reveal itself.

1.

2.

3.

God is our refuge and strength, an ever-present help in trouble. Therefore we will not fear, though the earth gives way and the mountains fall into the heart of the sea, though its waters roar and foam and the mountains quake with their surging. (Psalm 46:1–3)

Peace I leave with you; my peace I give to you. Not as the world gives do I give to you. Let not your hearts be troubled, neither let them be afraid. (Luke 14:27)

Now write down three *action* steps that you will and *must take* (works) to do your part in this.

1.

2.

3.

> But someone will say, "You have faith and I have works." Show me your faith apart from your works, and I will show you my faith by my works. (James 2:18)

Chapter

5

The Shoulder of a Strong Source

True Real-Life Experience

January 27, 2023
5:59 a.m.

    Faith is like a baby leaning totally on the shoulder of their parents. This picture is total dependence and trust that the shoulder that they are lying on is secure, safe, strong, and durable enough to hold their head. There is no doubt, nor ability to doubt.
    As I watch my son soundly asleep, resting his head on my shoulders, eyes close, and at times smiling as he sleeps on my shoulder, I realize that this child totally trusted that my shoulders were secure, safe, and dependent. I shed tears as I reminisced on how that must be how God wants us to trust and have faith in Him. He wants us to rest on His shoulder like this child, but yet in that moment, I realized I've failed in this act of faith.
    My arms began to hurt, yet still this child was comfortably asleep and smiling, still trusting. He did not know my arms were hurting. His only action was trusting that where he was lying was safe. He wasn't aware of his environment. His mind wasn't concerned with the time or that there was noise around. It all was blocked out. Even with the little

twitches he did in and out of sleep, his final position was resting on this shoulder comfortably.

Even when he changed positions and the shoulder grew tired, he trusted that there would be an arm ready to hold him. Total dependence on his source that has been placed in the form of a parent's arm.

As he grows, if this source is not reliable and as he lays on this source and *if* he were to be dropped with no security, he would cry. Slowly, the crying, with age, would become lack of trust; and then if he were to fall asleep, he would not trust the arm that once held him without hesitation.

I mentioned this other side of faith, referring to how we have not fully completely trusted our source (God) as a child would during our adult years.

I have lived my life by faith, but this great teacher puts it perfectly into words.

I received this revelation from an amazing teacher, Apostle Joshua Selman on February16, 2023 at 1:30a.m. when he asked, What does complete trust as an adult look like in our source?

- Recognizing that all things that are in line with your purpose takes limitations from your life.
- Recognize the presence of negativity that tells you, you cannot do what you have believe in your heart you can do.
- Believing what you believe will come to fruition.
- Foolishly believing without any reservation.

An example is a clock going round. When we see a working clock, we see the hand move around. What doesn't register to us is that the clock is being functioned by a battery. The clock can be very cheap or very expensive. The price doesn't matter because whether cheap or expensive, they both need one source to function, *a battery*. So the question to ask is in the line of a fiery faith that works is, What is or who is your source? Who is your battery?

My fiery faith works, despite me appearing crazy to others at the initial stages of my confessions. My source makes my positive confessions possible. My source, if you haven't recognized this by this point of the book, is the God of the heavens and creator of all things.

One thing I am sure of is that because I have a source, I can trust wholeheartedly. I rest assured knowing that my words, my ideas, and my competency really comes from the trustworthy source. I acknowledge this reassurance whatever the content of my faith produces.

Now this book is not telling you to believe what I believe or force you to believe in the God of the heavens and creator of all things. I am rather sharing evidence and experience that you may be able to give yourself the opportunity to choose for yourself the next course of your life on this earth. This book is meant to challenge each reader to ask themselves questions about the source (s) we have depended on, if they are reliable. If they are not reliable, then why will we continue to choose unreliable resources, making them to be the potent advocates of our belief systems, our lives, and generations to come? Why choose a poison to kill oneself every day when we are clearly not ready to die without a fulfilled purposeful life. For both believers of the gospel and unbelievers of the gospel of Jesus Christ, do not feel forced to choose my source. Be convicted to reexamine the source you have chosen. Is this source truly reliable to withstand any attack, to guide and help you live—truly live—beyond the physical? Below are some guided exercises to help us.

> Not that we are competent in ourselves to claim anything for ourselves, but our competence comes from God. (2 Corinthians 3:5 NIV)

> I can do all things through Christ Jesus who strengthens me. (Philippians 4:13)

Faith Exercise

What Source do you take your energy from?
Answer:

If someone or something (human or deity) were to challenge this source, can this source be challenged and lose or win?
Answer:

Can this source be taken away in any dimensional capacity?
Answer:

Does this source bring positive light to your mind, body, soul, and spirit?
Answer:

Look back at your answer and take a moment to ponder if your source is a reliable and trusting source.

If the answer is yes, then begin the challenge to know more about this source (research, books, videos, action steps, etc.). If the answer is no, then begin to challenge yourself to change the source of your life that will make your answer to the above question a yes!

Can your source be defeated by you (physically, mentally, emotionally, spiritually)?

Can your source be defeated by men/women?

Can your source fit in the compact of the human mind?

Can your source only be touched by human hands?

Can your source be defeated by another deity/source?

Chapter

6

Others

January 1, 2022
2:30 a.m.

Full. The house was full, as this great man was in town doing miracles and healing ailments of so many. It was heard that he could heal the sick, give sight to the blind, make the limb walk, and even raise the dead. So as he came to town, everyone was there to see him, even the people who did not like him. One house he visited was so packed. There was a group of friends that had a friend who could not walk his entire life. They desperately desired in their hearts for their friend to walk, but with a packed crowd surrounding the man who could do such a miracle without a doctor license, it seemed impossible to get to this man of miracles. So the friends did something "crazy" that no one else in that crowd saw coming. They asked the owner of the house a favor and he granted their favor, seeing what they wanted to do out of concern for their friend. They went up the side steps to the roof of the house, tore out anything that was in their way from out of the roof, created a rope, placed their friend in a sack-like thing, and began to lever him down in the middle of the roof that they had torn toward the man they felt was capable enough to heal their friend. Everyone was surprised. Some may have thought, *Seriously, this is foolish* or *What in the world are they doing?* But the man of miracles called this thing the friends did *"a great act of faith."*

In our terms, we would agree that this is a great example and true story of fiery faith, one that was made on behalf of their friend. They risked their lives and their reputation of what people will think of them. They believed on behalf of their friend.

I am so curious of what their friend who needed this healing was thinking as he watched his friends pull out the roof of a home and all that was done just to help him receive healing.

The man of miracle called this a great act of faith as the friends interceded for their friend, and the man of miracle healed the man as well as forgiving the man who was crippled by sins. This man of miracles was named *Jesus, the Christ*, Son of the heavenly God.

I came across this story and felt it would be a great way to continue this chapter! Kids are the most innocent and, without being affected by adults, are pretty genuinely honest and free-spirited humans. Others are very important in this world of humans floating around everywhere in this earth. Maybe this kid story will bring about some understanding of a visualized piece on fiery faith. When belief is in action of faith steps you meet answer prayers.

"Excuse Me, Sir, Do You Sell God?"
Little Boy and His Bottle of "God's Kiss"

Faced with setbacks in life, different people resort to different means to solve problems at hand, and those with faith go one step beyond surrendering to the divine, seeking his mercy. But is our faith truly unshakable? And do we truly, wholeheartedly believe that God is sheltering us from all adversities, at all times?

This tale is about a little boy who went around every shop in the hopes of finding a cure for his uncle and asked: "Do you sell God?"

The tale goes back to the time around the early 20th century, in a small town, somewhere in the Western United States where a 10-year-old boy held a penny in his hand and approached every shop owner along a street and asked: "Excuse me, Sir. Do you sell God?"

Thinking the boy was pulling a prank, store owners would chase him out. This was the general response he got throughout the day. However, the adamantly determined boy didn't give up. All day long, he walked in and out of stores seeking an opportunity to buy a little "God" with his humble penny.

As night fell, the little boy visited another store—it was the sixty-ninth shop—and repeated the same question to a silver-haired storekeeper: "Excuse me, Sir. Do you sell God here?"

The storekeeper, an old man, with a kind, gentle look in his eyes smiled and replied: "Tell me, child, why do you want to buy God?"

Finally, someone responded to the boy's question with compassion. Touched, and with tears rolling down his cheeks, the boy relayed his story to the storekeeper.

The boy's parents had passed away when he was still a toddler. And he lived with his loving uncle, who worked at a construction site. Unfortunately, his uncle had gotten injured at work and was unconscious. The doctors told the boy that only God could save his uncle. Hearing that, he thought God might be a wonderful thing and innocently believed: "If I buy some God and let my uncle eat a piece, his injuries will heal."

Tears welled up in the storekeeper's eyes as he listened to the boy's plight. "How much do you have?" he lovingly asked the child.

"A penny," the boy answered.

"Child, the price of God is exactly a penny!" he said.

The boy placed his precious penny in the storekeeper's hand, and the old man wasted no time in retrieving the magical bottle of "God's kiss" from the shelf. He gave the bottle to the child and said: "Take it, boy! When your uncle drinks this bottle of 'God,' he will be fine."

Ecstatic, he held "God" tightly in his arms and ran to the hospital as fast as he could.

"Uncle, I bought 'God' back and you will get well soon," the boy shouted joyfully to his uncle as he walked into the hospital ward.

The following day, a medical team visited the hospital to see patients including the little boy's uncle. Under their care and treatment, the boy's uncle gradually recovered. However, when the uncle saw the medical expenses marked as "paid," he was in disbelief. The hospital informed him that an elderly rich man had invited the team of doctors and had already settled the payment.

It turned out that the storekeeper who sold the bottle of "God's kiss" was a millionaire and enjoyed spending his free time at one of his stores. Excited, both the uncle and the young boy went to the shop to meet the man, but the owner was away and had left a letter for them. The message read:

"Sir, hope you are well. And you don't need to thank me. All the expenses have been paid by your nephew. I wanted to tell you that you are a lucky man to have such a good nephew. To save you, he brought a penny and went into every store he saw to buy 'God'... Thank God, and be grateful for your little nephew, as it was the child's faith that saved you!"

(Epoch Inspired Staff Time
February 10, 2023)

True Real-Life Experience

Faith is also waking up at 2:00 a.m. in the morning to intercede for your friend, who you see as trying so much in life to do the right thing and yet getting as though she's coming up short on and the feeling of failing is overwhelming overtaking her. Faith is trusting in the God you believe in to hear your prayers for her; to comfort, support, and bring a new light into her world.

The voice of God said to me, "I cannot allow you to take on the burden she has been given, but if you are willing, go with her in her car in person so that she would know that she is not alone. I am communicating with her through you. In the storm, I am in the boat with her. You don't have to say a word, just be there with her, plus you get to sleep in the car. Faith is believing this, my child."

True Real-Life Experience

Protecting your children from natural and spiritual harms will ignite fiery faith!

February 2, 2023
3:39 a.m.

A thick cloud with a big golden sword was coming toward me and hovering over the child lying in the bassinet. Trying to wake up but unable to move my body, I begin to pray in my spirit without physically moving my lips. I could hear the flow prayer by Bishop Dag Heward Mills that was put on prior to me sleeping playing in the midst. I was finally able to wake up and pray immediately along with the flow prayer, which was already praying against the devil of diseases and Beelzebub, the prince of devils. Bishop Dag was praying against demonic spiritual paralysis (Matthew 12:24).

Faith is waking up *suddenly* to pray against a dream and attacks against you and your children at 3:39 a.m. and believing your prayers are answered. You know this because after the prayer, there was a calmness afterward.

Faith Exercise

Have there been an instance where you were hoping that something would go well for a friend, a family member, or someone other than yourself? Have you felt the need to want to do something, but yet at times felt powerless and wasn't so sure what to do? Or did you do something, and it made the situation better?

Even the thought of thinking of someone else's well-being and hoping good for them without their knowing is enough. One way to ensure that that hope we have on behalf of another have a greater chance of occurring is through prayer.

Write the names of the people you are hoping good would come out of their situation. With faith in your heart, place the names of these individuals (like those friends who desperately wanted their friend to be healed and did not care how foolish they looked or who was watching them) in the prayer list below. I stand with you in this prayer.

1.

2.

3.

Heavenly Father, we thank you for the opportunity to call you Father and to call you Jehovah Rapha, the healer. In one accord, we believe in our hearts that you can heal_____ (insert name/s). So we lift these names unto you and ask for their situation to turn around for the better. We thank you for hearing and answering our prayer. In Jesus's name, we seal this and pray. Amen.

Chapter

7

Thoughts of Peace

January 7, 2023, Saturday
2:30–2:49 a.m.

> For I know the thoughts that I think toward you, saith the Lord, thoughts of peace, and not of evil, to give you an expected end. Then shall ye call upon me, and ye shall go and pray unto me, and I will hearken unto you. And ye shall seek me, and find me, when ye shall search for me with all your heart. And I will be found of you, saith the Lord: and I will turn away your captivity, and I will gather you from all the nations, and from all the places whither I have driven you, saith the Lord; and I will bring you again into the place whence I caused you to be carried away captive. (Jeremiah 29:11–14 KJV)

Thoughts of Peace

It is a peaceful thought to know that whatever you are looking for under the sun (the earth) is not something new. When I speak, I'm speaking of positive things, of course, because who in their right mind would want negative things to happen to them in this life? So let me put your mind to ease, understand that you were given exceeding great promises (2 Peter 1:4).

So when you are proclaiming things to happen by faith with belief in your heart, you're only stating what is already meant for you as promised.

True Real-Life Experience

January 7, 2023, Saturday
2:30–2:49 a.m.

What a week it has been, the spiritual intimacy I have had with the Lord through fasting and prayer.

The voice said, "This is my time with you."

I closed my eyes over and over again and saw a door.

The voice said, "The door is open."

Yet all I saw was a dark door. I closed my eyes again. Same thing.

I was then led to go to the life verse the Spirit gave me long ago, that I had almost come to forget. I went to Jeremiah 29:11, but I was led to read the King James Version. This is the version that is closest to the original scriptures out of all the versions that are now available on the Bible app. This, while listening to Victoria Orenze in the background on Thanksgiving.

I read the scripture, and to my surprise, I read a word that I did not remember seeing before in this verse: "thoughts of peace."

Then the inner man asked me, "Do you have peace?"

I began to say, "Forgive me, Lord, I have wronged you."

I began to weep in remorse and forgiveness.

"Forgive me, Lord, I have wronged you," I said over again.

The voice said, "It's okay, you did nothing wrong. I know your heart, and you only asked for financial prosperity because you want to glorify the Lord in your works. You want to give to the church by building a church. You want to help the little girl and save her by bringing her to you in the US. You want to have a home spacious enough to host meetings of sharing the Word. I want you to recognize it is not wrong to ask for financial blessings. Meanwhile, look at how far you have come and your life verse has been, and is, being fulfilled. Do not focus on the version that says, "prosper you," for I have prospered you through the original "peace that surpasses all understanding." I have given you all you need. I am with you and will remain with you."

In that moment, I saw my life verse Jeremiah 29:11 in a new light. It certainly had been fulfilled, and I do have peace.

I was led to close my eyes again, and this time, I saw the same door as before, but the darkness was now overcome by light.

I heard the same voice saying, "The door is open."

The lesson in this true encounter I am sharing is, let's really look at our present and how far you've come. Go back to that promise you felt God said to you. Which lens are you seeing it from? "Source of peace" or "Prosper you."

Could it be that they are one in the same or interchangeable?

3:00 a.m.

Playing Victoria Orenze's "I No Go Fear" song.

Faith Exercise

What are things that have been stressful for you presently?

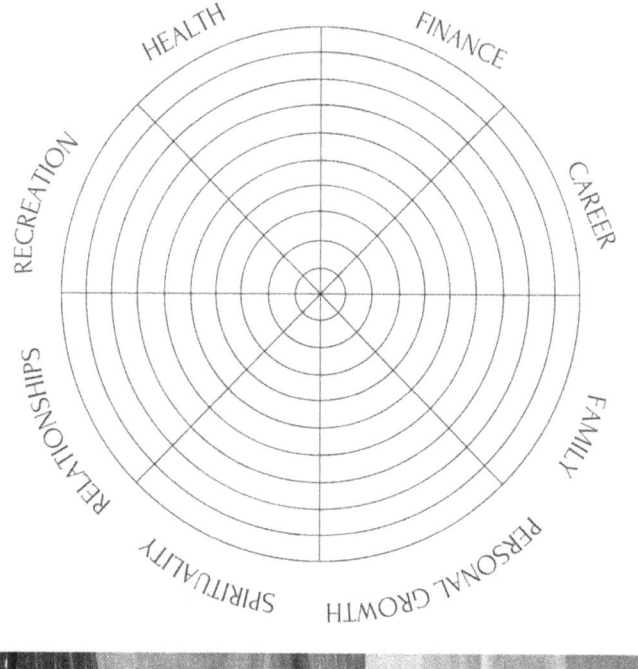

What makes them stressful physically, mentally, emotionally, spiritually?

What are some things that have been peaceful for you presently?

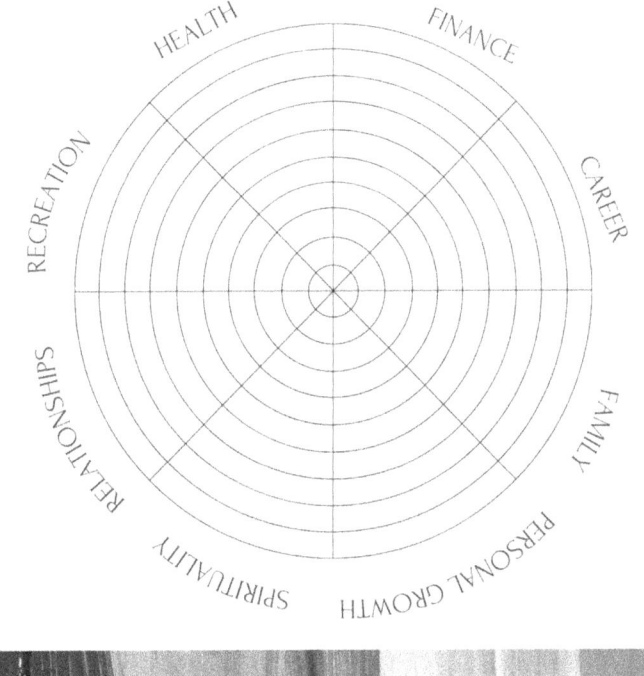

What makes them peaceful physically, mentally, emotionally, spiritually?
1. Write in the life wheel the level of stress from 0–10.
2. Now look at the lowest number. This one is encouraged to be the first item you work toward finding peace with. After peace is found, go to the next lowest number and so forth.
3. Think of how you obtained peace with the things you are already at peace with. Think of words you said to yourself to obtain peace with those things, thoughts you had or have that allows you a peaceful state, actions you completed that provide

you an environment to have peace with those things. Then utilize these same strategies with the things that are stressful as you move along the wheel. Some may be more difficult than the others to relate.

Chapter

8

Two Faith Aligned

Again I say unto you, That if two of you shall agree on earth as touching anything that they shall ask, it shall be done for them of my Father which is in heaven. For where two or three are gathered together in my name, there am I in the midst of them. (Mathew 18:19–20)

True Real-Life Experience

An evening I'll forever remember of not only strengthening my faith but allowing me to witness faith being manifested divinely in a marriage and in a man chosen by God.

My husband and I worshiped and prayed in faith together with Apostle Joshua Selman.

It was a four-hour-and-forty-six-minute service. I was in awe that my husband stayed the entire time and even took detailed notes on my behalf as I fed the baby.

I could see the tiredness in his eyes, so I asked him several times if he would like to go to sleep. I even reminded him that he had work tonight and he could go and nap for his 11:00 p.m.–7:00 a.m. shift. Each time he responded with, "I'm okay, it's okay." He continued with praying and listening to the message of "Open doors."

I truly believed in my heart that this must be God's doing.

He not only prayed but stood up to do so, answering back to the apostle. He was actively engaged. Toward the very end, he placed his arms around me as though giving me a big hug, and he prayed, summarizing our session of prayer. With a kiss, our fiery prayer time concluded.

I tell you the truth that what we prayed for and listed regarding the positive open doors that would happen in our lives was answered. We received the answers to the prayers we lifted up together that night. These were not just little topics; these were topics that would require a miracle to happen. But by us aligning together as one and sacrificially resisting sleep for that many hours, trusting our source of whom we were lifting the prayer topics to and believing in our hearts fervently signed, our prayers were all answered.

My husband also later testified that, that night when he went to work, despite him being awake for our prayer session, he was more awake at work and had a productive time at work.

Another real-life event occurred when I traveled out of state to visit my mother L., who had just had a procedure done to help cure meningitis symptoms. My second mother G. took both my children with me (a three-month-old and a toddler). We traveled with a car that had an engine light on and no working horn. It was an urgent trip. Yet the miracle began when I was obedient to remain at the home of my second mother for the majority of the trip. I was there for about two weeks, traveling from one home to the other, using the same car without a horn. The horn was checked throughout the trip, and it still was not working. The day of my return home, it began to rain. Mother G and I prayed as she asked me to lead the prayer. I prayed accordingly in alignment with her. We prayed for safety. The children and I departed. The rain began to fall harder as a heavy New York truck began to take over the road over my regular size car with two babies in it. I then stopped at a service center as I was getting really sleepy. I closed my eyes and slept in the car with the children. After about fifteen minutes, I suddenly woke up, and my arms hit the horn of the car accidentally. I heard a noise, so I looked outside. At this time, the rain had stopped. There was no other car around me, so I then touched my car's horn, and low and behold, it was working. The sound of the horn was completely different from the original sound. Until this very day, it remains changed. I immediately called Mother G. to express the miracle that happened with the car horn.

She stated, "To God be the glory, as we were praying when you were here, the car horn was in my heart for y'all to get home safely. When y'all left, it was on my heart still, and I lifted a prayer for y'all that everything on the car will begin to work."

I thanked her and thanked God for aligning our prayer request and answering it. The children and I came home from out of state safely.

Another situation: My best friend had received a letter stating she was *not matched* into a pediatrician residency program after eight years of medical school. Here's a glimpse of her testifying what alignment did for her:

I Am (Finally) Going to Be a Pediatrician!!!!

>Pediatrics has always been my passion; my aspiration and calling since I was a little girl. The road has been long and tumultuous, but I persisted. After an intense application and interview season, I was shocked to find out that I didn't Match or #SOAP into a pediatric residency program. I was devastated.
>
>Years of hard work, determination and perseverance seemed to all go down the drain. This felt like the lowest blow, however, I did not lose hope. I knew what God said about me (Jeremiah 29:11) and I refused to give up! I went back into prayer mode and my prayer army went to war on my behalf (don't play with us, mmkay!). There was no way I was going to come this far to only come this far! I completely surrendered to God's plan, and allowed him to move in and through me. What seemed to be a bleak situation, turned into a glorious event!
>
>A few days later, I got the call of a lifetime. Now with a grateful heart, I'm happy to announce that I will be joining THE amazing pediatric team at the University of Tennessee Health Science Center!! In this

incoming class (Peds and Med/Peds), I am 1 of a 5 IMGs, with 3 of us hailing from Ross SOM 🐶 All glory belongs to God alone! I'm so honored to train at an amazing program with great support and can't wait to meet my co-residents!

The testimony is heavy and means so much to me. We won y'all! God has won the victory! To my husband who covered me, family who supported me, mentors who pushed me (thank you Dr. Williams!) and sisters who spoke life into me: THANK YOU!!! 🥹💜

God is glorified, fam! Please join me in dancing like David danced! Be encouraged that whatever God has said about you will come to pass! A delay is never a denial!

These real life alignment expresses that in the moments of fiery faith when one cannot gather the strength to move out of an unhealthy or stressful situation, leaning on others and agreeing in one accord to connect to the aligned source, changes will occur. As one is on fire the moment you get in close proximity, the fire becomes upon whatever is in close proximity .

Believing and Faith Are *Not* the Same Thing

On December 28, 2023 at 7:00 p.m., as I listened to Kathryn Coleman on the message of faith, I learned that faith comes from God himself. Scripture tells us that "God is the author and finisher of our faith." He gives faith, and he says all we need is a mustard seed of it. Because believing is not faith. For example, if I have a watch and give it to you as a Christmas gift, it becomes your watch. Yet the watch first belonged to me before it was given to you as a gift to belong to you. So if someone sees you with the watch, they won't say, "Ooh, I like the watch Rebekah gave you." They will say, "I like *your* watch," referring to it being yours. But only you know that it was given to you by Rebekah. Yet by it being on you, you are manifesting that you appreciate and like the gift for others to see. In the same way, when faith is given to us by

God himself, we should outwardly profess and live in action by faith. This then grow the curiosity of others who may not yet know God as their creator and giver of faith. They would say, "I like your watch-faith," or for a more practical way, they may say, "Wow, you really have faith." Then it opens the door to receive, and a conversation on how you got the faith you have will start. It also opens a conversation for you to give the glory to the original giver of the gift (God) that you are expressing.

Believing and faith are *not* the same thing. Even the devil believes that there is a God because he knows who created him originally as the angel Lucifer. We can believe something, but not have faith in it because faith comes from God himself. In the worldly view of things, you and I can believe that we will lose weight. But if you take the action steps in losing weight and all you do is believe you could do the same in your mind, then your belief remains a belief. In order for us to receive the gift of faith, we must receive God himself in human form, through Jesus Christ as our Lord and Savior, and live in action in and of that which we believe.

Faith counteracts the plans of the enemy.

One night, on January 4, 2024, at 1:57 a.m., I was sitting in the beautiful dining room of our new home after hosting a family gathering, while the two babies were asleep. I looked around me, and my heart was filled with gratitude. The only thing I could say was "Thank you, Lord." I was thinking of my faith that at some point was so low that it depleted hope and belief not only in God but also in myself, in my will to live. I allowed the mustard seed that God placed in my life to dry out. From a very young state, at a very young age, my environment concluded that faith was at a far distance.

I thought as I was in this dining room, *The enemy wanted to kill all this harvest, these blessings, this life and the life of four others (the children and my husband) and many more (the lives of the many people that has been reached through me a vessel, to believe and live a life in Christ Jesus). Yet, because we as humans are not the giver of faith, we only receive faith and are trusted to grow our faith daily, the one who gave me faith on that night when my hope was lost and I attempted to take this breath in me away in an action of suicide, He kept me from doing so. To this day it's but a miracle. I could have hindered all this newfound blessings from happening. I would have killed not just my own, but many lives by taking my own.*

Faith needs our attention even in the times of hardship. It is but grace (the unmerited side of grace, not earned side) that even when we cannot see the future and the hope that lies ahead, the one who gives faith still is with us. Did He still see that mustard seed in me years ago? I certainly could never have imagined my life would be this beautiful by grace.

Yet it is hard to see when we decide not to believe in Him. Which is why this book is written to encourage those who are missing out on a greater life experience because of unbelief and to ask to those who says they believe to check if they are living in actions steps of their belief.

Jesus said to him, "If[a] you can believe, all things are possible to him who believes." Immediately the father of the child cried out and said with tears, "Lord, I believe; help my unbelief!" (Mark 9:23–25).

Action-Step Prayer

Please forgive me, Lord, for trying to kill all of these people, as I attempted to kill myself through the loss of my faith in you, forgetting the seed in which you planted. Please help me in my unbelief to believe and move in faith action steps, in Jesus's name, Amen.

Your turn.

Please forgive me, Lord, for *(insert items of disbelief you have done or thought of)* through the loss of my faith in you, forgetting the seeds in which you planted. Please help me in my unbelief to believe and move in faith action steps, in Jesus's name, Amen.

Chapter

9

What We Hear

January 4, 2023
1:43 a.m.

Faith comes by hearing and hearing the word of God. The "word" of God is not only written in the pages of the sixty-six books of the Bible. God's word is alive and still speaking through his Holy Spirit. As he *speaks* His word to you, to us, we practice faith by believing what he is saying. We practice faith by responding in a dialogue conversation with him and taking action steps to whatever instructions the word tells us. In this case, following the biblical words that have already been spoken from God. Faith without works is dead. You must speak it to hear yourself, as faith comes by hearing.

Faith Exercise

But what does it say? "The word is near you; it is in your mouth and in your heart. That is the message concerning faith that we proclaim." (Romans 10:8 NIV)

Step 1

What are some statements and words you've said to yourself that you wish you could take back?

_____
_____
_____
_____
_____
_____
_____

Step 2

Now with a pencil or a pen cross out these words/statements. Then close the book and come back another time (at least after one hour). It is highly encouraged to not read the next instructions until you return.
Stop if you have not taken time away.

Step 3

Rewrite statements that are opposite to the ones you've written above. For the once you do not remember the exact wording because you've erased them physically, create new statements/words:

_____
_____
_____
_____
_____
_____
_____

Step 4

Say each new statement that is written in step 3 out loud to yourself three times.

Congratulations, you have planted a faith seed of newness and light in your being. Now to ignite the fire, it will take you believing in your heart what you have spoken with your mouth. You can water this seed you planted today by proclaiming it every day with fresh water, connecting it like a water hose to your source.

True Real-Life Experience

2023 Theme Word

At 12:40 a.m., I was listening to Victoria Orenze, Nathaniel Bassey, and Dunsin in Oyekan "See How Far You've Brought Me" song ministration on YouTube.
"The door is open."
When I first heard this, I was excited. The thoughts that this year open doors meant many blessings flowing in. Then I kept hearing this "open door" the next day and began to take it more seriously to its meaning. I heard a voice saying with the blessings will come attacks because the door is open. It allows both blessings and other things to come in, which would mean that I would *need* to pray consistently to prevent any other things that aren't blessings from coming in. They aren't curses, but with every blessing, there is a chance the enemy will attack, but my prayers will ignite the heavens to fight on my behalf.
After hearing this, I became weary and afraid that I wasn't up to the task to pray consistently. I wanted to receive the blessings that I longed for and prayed for, especially the financial breakthrough. I had to ask myself if I trust myself to hold my end of this deal (as I saw it). I even began to doubt that it was from God, because I thought, *If God wanted to bless me this year, he wouldn't give me this task where the blessings depended on me and my prayers to prevent interference from the enemy.* I started saying, "Lord, I don't know if I want this open door anymore. I cannot put the children and marriage at risk just because I want blessings to

pour in our lives through this open door. I don't trust myself to pray every time, or even enough to fight against the enemy. I don't know what he may do to the kids to cause illness or worse just for blessings…"

I'm thinking that I've really only prayed fervently for financial breakthrough. There's nothing wrong with praying for this, but it's not worth the risk. I am already blessed, and I choose to be content.

The voice said, "You have time before you make your final decision."

At this moment, my oldest son that God gave me was ill (eyes discharge, coughing, temperature of 103 degrees). Fear began to overtake me, and I said to myself or maybe it was to the voice.

"Yeah, I'm not willing to have things like this happen just for blessings."

Then in my spirit, I was led to take water and pray over it and give it to the child.

You see, in the past, the child wouldn't drink much water. He would only take a sip. But I did it anyway. I took his sipping cup, poured the water in it halfway, prayed over it for healing and pleaded the blood of Jesus with faith and belief in my heart, and brought it to him. He surprisingly immediately took it from me and began to drink it. I watched him in curiosity if he would actually drink all of that water.

The voice said, "Do not fear. Push fear aside."

So I did and watched fervently as my child drank. He wanted to stop, I thought, but then it felt like an angel's hand kept the sipping cup to his mouth. He drank all the water, every last sip. There was a little left in the cup toward the end. I said to myself as I watched him, "If he drinks all this water, then yeah, this is definitely from God."

He drank it all, without my interference, his hand never left that sipping cup until all the water was gone.

I grabbed him and thanked God for healing.

Not too long after, he fell asleep and was placed in his bed to sleep. The next day there was no discharge on his face, and his temperature went down.

The voice then said, "All you need to do is pray like this."

January 4, 2023
12:55 a.m.

    Prior to this, I wanted to be in full-time ministry as a youth shepherd/ young life leader.

    I don't want to be mediocre in this work, I am ready for this door to be open and do what is needed. I want this to transform me, radical transformation, thankful to being used through this open door.

    I had said this in fear of what might come through the open door, but after this situation, my response was "Let your will be done, your good and perfect will. I trust you Lord. I don't trust myself to pray or pray enough when blessings come with the enemy attack attached to it, but I do trust you and your will. I am content with what I have, and I trust that you provide *all* of my needs as you always have, so I give it all to you, whether the door is open or close, I give it to your will, which I know your will is good. I don't want the door. I want what you have."

    Turns out that day and night, the prayers that I said I couldn't do or didn't trust myself to do I found myself praying in God's presence for hours to the point where I fell asleep in his presence.

    I was still happy with my decision to give up the door for God's will. In my heart, I felt I was focusing on the financial blessings coming through that door, something I longed for, but it was not worth putting my family at risk.

    I looked around me and said, "I am blessed already. I will do my very best to pray and remain in your presence, Lord. I just don't want it to be dependent on the door. I refuse to give the enemy any opportunity. (Written on January 4, 2023, at 1:35 a.m.)

> Now without faith, it is impossible to please God, since the one who draws near to him must believe that he exists and that he rewards those who seek him. (Hebrews 11:6)

So we've come close to the end of this book. Here are my final words to all of this: If you have not experienced a change in the desire to have fiery faith and connect to a mighty good source, I want to encourage you that there is a reward that comes with having fiery faith. Who doesn't like to be rewarded? The cool part about the heavenly source is that He is such a source of justice that He states He has already given a mustard seed of faith to *everyone*! Whether you are a believer in Christ Jesus or not, you who are reading this book have this mustard seed. So a reward is waiting for you. The only catch to all of this is "the one who draws near to this mighty source must believe that He exists." Honestly, that seems fair right? Like why expect a gift or reward from someone who you do not even believe has the ability to reward you. It wouldn't make sense. Rewarding is a divine and human thing.

Why do men reward men? We walk by motivation. Rewards make us work harder. For example, if a parent has two children in the home and if one child believes that if a chore is done that their parent has a reward for them and therefore goes about doing the chore, trusting that the parent will do what he said, in expectation, the child completes the chore. To maintain the trust and relationship with the child, even if the parent does not have something on hand, that parent is now obligated to reward the child and stick to the words that were said to the child. Meanwhile, the child who did not believe the words of the parent and did not believe the parent's ability to reward rejected the opportunity of ever being rewarded or creating an obligation to the parent to reward him/her.

Well, as you have read all of these real-life testimonies and outcomes, the source in which I am speaking of says these words of rewarding those who seek Him in faith and belief in their heart words has never gone void. Therefore, I encourage you to give yourself the opportunity to be rewarded for what is already in you: "a faith seed." Allow that faith seed to be watered into the *fiery faith*, believing that God is real, and He will reward you, never leaving you nor forsaking you.

> Now without faith, it is impossible to please God, since the one who draws near to him must believe that he exists and that he rewards those who seek him. (Hebrews 11:6)

Your steadfast faith will bring you a reward. It is okay to expect a reward. As a man named Paul expected a reward for being steadfast in fighting for his faith, as he stated, "I have fought a good fight of faith, I expect a reward" (2 Timothy 4:6–8).

Similarly, a boy named David, who fought a giant man when this giant beast was threatening the people of Israel. The king stated whoever slayed this giant will be rewarded these things: his daughter and being free of tax (1 Samuel 17:24, David and Goliath). David had his own motivation as to why he must slay the giant, one being he had God, his source guiding him. To the king, it didn't matter what David's motivation was as long as the giant was slayed. The king had to do what he promised, to reward any man that slayed the giant.

> In as much as mere men and kings who are obligated to keep their words, imagine what the God of the universe must be obligated to do by what he says he will do. So be reminded of these words and remind the source of his words as you choose to work on obtaining fiery faith. God's character is a giver…a rewarder…he is the rewarder, so shall you be rewarded as you do this "Now without faith, it is impossible to please God, since the one who draws near to him must believe that he exists and that he rewards those who seek him. (Hebrews 11:6)

In the next and final chapter are true life testimonials from others who have received such rewards by taking this tiny mustard seed that was initially given to them and decided to water it with baby steps of drawing nearer to their source, with belief in their heart that he truly rewards them for what they can now understand to be *fiery faith*!

May the impartation of fiery faith be caught by you as you read these true-life testimonies of others just like you and I.

PS It is okay to be crazy—oops, we said "fiery"—as long as you have the right source backing you.

Chapter

10

Fiery Faith Moments of Others

Dr. Erika Tabiri-Nketia: Fire-Blazing, Life-Breathing Faith

> For truly I tell you, if you have faith the size of a mustard seed, you will say to this mountain, "Move from here to there," and it will move; and nothing will be impossible for you." (Matthew 17:20–21)

In a sermon entitled "The Power of Unbelief" by Dr. Tony Evans, I've come to learn that "faith the size of a mustard seed" isn't necessarily referring to the dimensions of the seed, but rather the *life* within.

Since I was a little girl, I have desired to be a pediatrician. I did not know how, but I had hope that it was going to happen. I've had to use life-breathing, fiery faith throughout my entire premed and medical school journey. More recently, I used fiery faith in the area of passing the United States Medical Licensing Exams (USMLE). For graduation requirements, medical students are required to pass both Step 1 and Step 2 to assess our basic and clinical knowledge skills, respectively. Though I passed Step 1 on the first try, Step 2 was a daunting mountain, standing between my diploma and I. I studied for countless hours, did hundreds of questions, solidified concepts with my study partner, took exam preparation classes, performed well on many assessments; yet I did not pass on the first try. Through tears, I overcame anxiety and defeat, changed my study tactics, and increased my prayer and fasting lifestyle. A sense of peace overwhelmed me. God had my back. I attempted the exam again, only to find out I missed it by a few points yet again! In total, it took me four tries to finally pass the exam—the maximum amount allowed! It was only by the grace of God that I passed on my last and final try.

Due to test anxiety and past failures, I was afraid to apply to pediatric residency programs believing the lie that I was no longer worthy of becoming a doctor. Fortunately, God had better plans, as He promises in Jeremiah 29:11. With a newfound mindset change and confidence boost, I applied to many residency programs across the nation. After a long, brutal interview season, one program director offered me a position to train as a pediatric resident at a well-known resourced program! I believed in God and myself, and in turn, they believed in me. I'm forever grateful to God for this trial by fire which ignited my faith. Thanks to my support system (husband, family, sisters in Christ, and mentors), I am now one step closer to becoming a board-certified pediatrician. To God be all the glory!

Mrs. Captain Natalie Kadie Fasan

It amazes me how having faith in God requires a seed that only He can provide. We learned that we are given a measure of faith as small as a mustard seed, but without the gift of faith, we wouldn't be able to believe in Him. Insert song break. "For from you are all things, and to you are all things… you deserve the glory." As much as I can share about my personal experience with faith, I'm mostly grateful for the fiery faith of my loved ones that believed for me when I couldn't.

I'm sure by now we've all encountered someone whose name didn't always bring laughter and joy.

I was once that girl.

I was once the girl who couldn't seem to do anything right.

I was once the girl who disobeyed authority and hated correction.

I don't think you have enough time to read about my juvenile delinquency, but I'll share an encounter with fiery faith that still blows my mind.

It was about thirteen years ago when I made the brave decision to join the Army. I was seventeen years old with no plans of attending college traditionally. Instead, I walked up to the Army recruiter who visited my high school and told him to sign me up.

As anxious as I was to leave my mother's house, my actions said otherwise. I continued to get in fights, and right before graduation, an incident caught up with me. I was scheduled for community service and at risk of missing my ship date for basic training. My mother's faith and prayers remained consistent.

At a final court appearance where the defender recommended, I admitted to things I didn't commit, a uniformed man appeared at the courthouse to represent me. This man was the commander of the Army recruiting station, and he *never* made a court appearance on behalf of a recruit before. He showed up for me. GOD showed up for me.

As much as I wanted to change my life and make better decisions, I needed an advocate to defend me and give me a second chance. My mother's faith spoke for me when I couldn't see or believe for myself. Sometimes the faith of your loved ones or destiny helpers will intercede for you, and God honors that as well. Now, I can honestly see I'm a much better woman who knows the power of faith for myself, but especially for those who are incapable of believing for themselves.

Mrs. Julia Baptista-Clement
(Deacon)

The author of this book was instructed by God to ask me to write a time when my burning faith was evident. This is an extraordinary life event I had the privilege of experiencing. Allow me to start at the beginning.

I am a deacon at my church and have been for the past ten years. In the role as deacon, I serve as armor bearer for the pastor and servant to the congregation. At the start of each Sunday service, there's an invocation. A time of prayer dedicated to inviting the Holy Spirit to join us. Members in the congregations are extended an opportunity for individual prayer. The deacons go about the sanctuary to those with their hands raised and anoint them with oil and enter into prayer with them. Some may share what it is that's pressing on their hearts; others may not. Our job is to meet each person where they are. We enter into this agreement with the will of God. Not our thoughts or intentions, but His. On this particular Sunday, a young woman raised her hand and caught my attention. I walked over to anoint her with oil, and this is what transpired.

As soon as she was anointed and we clasped hands, I began to hear pastor's voice in the distance. I came to realize that our consciousness, our essence, our spirits were no longer in the sanctuary. We were in the great void, the time prior to the earth being formed. God's voice was heard speaking these words: **"She hears with my ears, she sees with my eyes, and she speaks with my mouth."** I was completely taken back, speechless, and awestruck. I have been moved by God in the past. He has a way of impressing His will upon your heart to the point that you think you're hearing Him, but it's not audible. This time, however, it was different. I must admit that there was no fear, no anxiousness, *only peace*. I found myself not wanting this time to end. I wanted to continue to bask in His presence. When we eventually returned, broke our embrace, she shared that she would be traveling out of the country and really needed to hear from Him, needed to obtain His blessing. The words from Isaiah 55:8–9 was profound this day.

> For My thoughts are not your thoughts,
> Nor are your ways My ways," declares the Lord.
> For as the heavens are higher than the earth,
> So are My ways higher than your ways
> And My thoughts than your thoughts.

Little did I know that this young woman would become so precious to me, a special gift from God: The daughter I didn't give birth to. Father God, I am so grateful to have been used in this fashion. May this life event be an encouragement to those who are seeking you.

Ms. Evelyn Williams
(A Mother, Caregiver)

On April 30, 1995, my first son was born, a day where my heart was overjoyed yet my mind was worried about the current civil war that was at a high peak in my country Liberia. We survived his first year. During the year 1996, on his first birthday he became really sick and had an internal illness that was unknown to me. The situation of the country became even more dire where, at this time, there was no food, proper drinking water or sustainable safety. Despite this situation we were surviving. I had heard about God but was not a full-on believer and did not practice and form of faith. So when my son became sick my reliance was on myself and others to help me. His sickness was not normal. I walked about 15 minutes to a place called Grace stone that I had heard had medical personnels there aiding people who were shot or wounded by the war. He was at this time critically ill to the point of death. He smelled, boils were over his body. I reached the place and found a red cross at this location. There were three other babies there that were also ill. I quickly asked the medical personnel to help me, they took one look at my child and I and stated that my child was already dead, their words "during the war we are trying to help people who already have life." At this time, I was unsure what to do. One of the mothers of the children at this place said that they said her child will not make it if the child does not have a certain medication and she does not have any money for the medication. Forgetting about my current troubles with my son who has already been deemed as "dying", I remembered a good Samaritan gave me $50.00USD a week prior and this was my last money I had to provide for food for my son and me. Yet I gave this mother who needed medication to treat her child as her child was also ill. She appeared even more distraught to have her child revived from sickness. They had deemed that her child was revivable. Despite my child being lifeless as they told me, I had to give her this to give her hope as well. She took the money and the medical personnels provided her with medical treatment, yet still the two babies who were deemed by the medical personnels as having more life unfortunately passed away.

My son remained with me at this facility for the night, due to the ongoing killing and shooting in the surrounding areas. At daylight I walked again 25 minutes to another clinic called Sweden Relief hoping that they will help my child. My son at this time is defecating, urinating as I walk. The doctors continue to tell me "This baby is dead, go home until he takes his final breath". I left and met a good Samaritan, who then provided me with a wrap and chlorine water and I used this to wash my child in it. At this time, I honestly did not know much about God.

I still felt in my heart that I did my best, and then I said "God, I don't know if you are real, but if you are I tried my best, Here is my child. If he will live, let him live, if he will die here, here he is.

Somehow, I still had "zeal" in me, I then went home with my child and got some earthly roots with greens from the African soil, made a remedy and placed it on him. We went to sleep, my child started getting swollen, his eyes shut close, he had no movements. A praying woman came and prayed for me and the child that night. She stated that in the morning we would go and bury him.

I did not cry, somehow I did not know how to conclude this situation. Something in me knew he would live. (I later found out this something was the holy spirit), if he went among children who they said would live and he was already dead, yet he did not die then, and still had some breath in him up to now. I did not have any fear in me anymore. I went back and told God again, if you are real, show me you are, this child is a gift to me, his name is God's gift, you gave him to me, so if you let him live or let him die, he will still end up coming to you. Let "Gift" live.

My son Gift Gargar Williams is now 29 years old, married with a home and business in America. Fully alive and fully serving God.

I went from being a person who had no relationship with God, no prayer r any conversation with him. To me now knowing yes indeed, there is a God, a supreme being somewhere that hears when you call, my faith grew, my fiery faith. Even when we don't acknowledge him he is there, so when we do come to realize his presence all along, our eyes can truly see he's been there this whole time. My faith will never be the same. There have been truly many other moments of fiery faith since then, and I thank God almighty for igniting my faith every time.

My dark rooms days have been made into days of light ...a story that is ongoing.

Anonymous

It was 1998, I was eighteen years of age. I, a senior in high school and working full-time second shift in one of the local factories that my mother also worked for, Paramount Cards, where we made greeting cards. Now throughout my childhood, I suffered with migraine headaches. In and out of emergency rooms and seeing specialists from Providence to Boston, no doctor could explain why I was having these headaches. This prevented me from participating in most physical activities like joining sports teams and activities a young boy would enjoy. Now as a teenager without the structure or discipline I would have experienced playing on sports teams, I gravitated toward the wrong groups of friends. Getting into trouble with the law here and there, nothing too serious, but this was just the beginning. Then at the age of eighteen, I woke up one morning with a headache like no other, the headache of all headaches. This one was different from all the others. I tried to carry on my normal activities, but no matter what medication I took, this headache would not let up. This went on for four days, each day worse than the prior. On the fourth day, while at work, I bent over to pick something up. And as I arose, I became extremely dizzy, and my eyesight became blurry. Now my heart rate began to speed up, and I started to freak out. I thought, maybe I'm having one of those anxiety attacks my mother always talks about, something that runs in my family but have never experienced. I made my way to the bathroom splashing my face with water, talking to myself in the mirror, "Michael, calm down. You're just having an anxiety attack." As I'm looking at myself, I notice my head is moving, pulsating. I can see my head moving in an unnatural manner. I became extremely scared and began to run to my mother's office. This is the last thing I remember. My mother says I opened her office door, and before I could say the word "ambulance," I collapsed. I came to, and I was being rushed down a hospital hallway surrounded by doctors and people in white jackets, one of them screaming, "We need to get him into surgery. He is bleeding in the brain."

Now before they can open my head, a test needs to be done. This test revealed the bleeding had stopped. Just stopped, which is unheard of. At this point, opening my skull was not necessary. The blood that had leaked from what was a blood clot needed to be drained to release the pressure crushing my brain. Going through an artery in my thigh, they drained the blood that leaked in my skull. The blood clot had formed on the part of the brain that gives strength and feeling to the left side of my body. The doctors had no reason for how the bleeding stopped, but I knew how it happened, so I told them. It was my God. He responded, saying, "Truly you are blessed because 97 percent of people who have this happen to them die immediately."

So once I become stable again, the conversation of how to move forward needs to be had. With my family and doctors at the table, they explained to us the effects of removing this blood clot. Because of where the clot is located, removing it can result in death, or if you're lucky, you make it through, but the left side of your body will be paralyzed.

"If you're lucky," he says, "it will be just your leg, or just your arm, just your face. But through my experience of forty years, I'm telling you by performing this surgery the left side of your body will be paralyzed, but because you're so young, I believe there's another route we can take. If you take blood thinners for an extended period of time, the blood clot can dissolve and go away on its own."

We decided to go with the blood thinners to see if the blood clot would dissolve on its own. After nine months of being bed stricken and monitored by doctors, the clot was not growing but wasn't dissolving either. The doctors suggest I get out of bed and start getting back into living life again.

"Little steps," they say. "You're still young enough to finish high school. Start with going back to school and take it from there."

It didn't take long for me to pick up where I left off: chasing pretty girls around and hanging in the streets. I met a beautiful Cape Verdean girl who became the love of my life, or so I thought. It wasn't long before she was pregnant. With no high school diploma or any particular skill set, I had no way to support a family, so I decided to attend a trade school by the name of Job Corps, where I could obtain a GED and get certified in a trade in order to support my new family. Eleven days into my Job Corps experience, I was arrested and arraigned on sixty years to serve in prison. Long story short, I served nine months in county jail, five hundred miles away from anyone I knew. All I had was God. The stress of my girlfriend being pregnant and me not being there for her, trying to survive in jail, the fights, and constantly wondering if the blood clot would leak again. By the grace of God, I never had so much as a headache, no seizures, nothing. With no medication, no doctors, just my faith and prayer.

Now it's been a little over a year since I have had any kind of check up on my head since the surgery. While in jail, I was refused any kind of treatment related to my prior brain aneurysm. Upon my release, I didn't have health insurance in order to see a doctor, let alone see a specialist or get an MRI. My girlfriend was working as a secretary for a doctor, she explained my situation to the doctor, and he got me in for an MRI the very next day, again, by the grace of God. It was a Tuesday morning. We did the MRI, and I was told someone would contact me by Thursday with the results. My phone rang at 8:00 a.m. the very next morning.

Mr. Duarte, you need to contact your neurologist immediately. The blood clot is 4 cm bigger than it was when it erupted.

Once my surgeon received the imaging, he says, "Michael, you have two options here. Option one, surgically remove the clot, which is an extremely sensitive and delicate surgery. Your head will be open for eight hours. There are many things that could go wrong. While I'm in your head with my knife, if an eyelash falls off my face and lands on the knife, you will die. Option two, live with this blood clot in my head, monitoring it regularly. But the clot could erupt at any time. Simply picking up your child, and the rush to the brain could cause it to erupt. You're crossing the street, and a car almost hits you and you jump back and flinch, it could cause it to erupt, and you can die."

Example, after example, he is going on and on and in all circumstances I would die. As I'm listening to him, I'm not listening to him, I'm talking to the Lord because from the sounds of things, I can't do anything about this and neither can this doctor. This will be decided by God himself. The Lord will guide this doctor's mind and hands toward what the Lord's will is for my life. The doctor says to take the time I need to figure out what route I want to go with this.

At this point, there is only one piece of advice that I'm looking for, and that's God himself. I needed to be in the Lord's house. I wasn't attending any particular church at the time, but I remembered a church my mother had taken me to years prior where we heard a choir by the name of Prism of Praise. Of all the churches I've ever been to throughout my life, I'd never felt the spirit of God like I did at this church. So, in searching for a conversation with God, I drove directly to the church formerly known as 4th Baptist Church on Hope Street in Providence, RI. Today the church is known as Mount Hope Community Baptist Church, MHCBC.

I went to the altar and fell to my knees.

"Father, you brought me in this world, and you will take me out. Father, I have a decision to make, and I don't know which to choose. What would you have me do? I need your guidance. I need you to tell me what you want me to do. Is this my fate? Is this where I die? If so, help me to accept that. Father, I need you to tell me what to do. Do I have the surgery, or do I live with this blood clot in my head? I need a clear, straightforward answer from you, Father. Tell me what to do."

For the first time in my life, I brought something to the altar and left it there. I didn't take the worry with me. I left it at the altar and got up off my knees with no fear at all. It was such an amazing feeling. I could feel fear and worry being stripped from me. I then went home, sat in my favorite recliner, and put the TV on. As I'm watching TV, a commercial for the nightly news comes on and goes something like this: "Tonight's exclusive story, the ten top neurologists in New England."

"This is amazing," I said to myself. "I'm going to watch this to see if my neurologist is on this list."

My doctor was no. 2 out of 10 on this list. I took this as an answered prayer. I believed God was telling me not to worry to go through with the surgery and have full faith in the doctor.

And that is what I did.

My mother and I sat with the doctors and said we are going through with the surgery. The doctor looks at my mother and says, "I suggest you have your vehicle and your home-made wheelchair accessible because your son is going to be paralyzed."

Fiery FAITH

My mother responded to him, "I'm not doing that. I feel I would be speaking it into existence by doing that. No. If it happens, then I'll do it."

As I said my final farewells to my family before going into surgery.

My older brother whom I had never seen cry before said to me, "How come you look so calm. Aren't you scared?"

"No, I'm not scared. This is in God's hands, whatever his will is, will be. God is in control."

So the options going into this surgery were as such, I would die on the table in surgery or, two, the left side of my body would be paralyzed. If I'm lucky, it would be just my leg or just my arm, or just my face.

The surgeon says, "Through my forty years' experience in doing this, Mr. Duarte, if you make it through this surgery, the whole left side of your body will be completely paralyzed."

I was in the operating room. The gas mask was put over my face, and I was told to count back from ten. Ten…nine…and that's all I remember. I woke up ten hours after the surgery was complete. I was alone when I came to. My head felt like it wanted to explode, and I had to pee like never before. Disoriented, I needed to find a bathroom. I gathered all the tubes hanging out of me and made my way to the hallway. I could see the nurses at the end of the hall all at the nurses' station. One nurse said to another, "Is that Duarte down there?"

"No way," the other responded, "He just got out of surgery. Oh my God, it is Duarte."

And they all started running toward me. They grabbed me and led me back to my bed.

"What are you doing? You need to be in bed, you just got out of surgery."

"I need to pee," I said.

"You have a catheter."

I said, "I don't know what that means, but I need to pee."

She explained what a catheter is.

We all have a good laugh, and by the grace of God, I'm not paralyzed.

Mrs. Jasmine Kefel
(RN and Doctor of Dentistry Candidate)

When desperation and the word of God collides. Desperation in the sense that I had exhausted all of my resources. I had gone above and beyond in my own strength to do everything I was physically able to do. And when I had done all that I could, I had to rely on the supernatural power of God to turn my situation around. In 2020, during a tumultuous year where COVID has delayed the reunion of me and my husband, our infant child having not met her father since birth, me struggling as a new mother trying to navigate motherhood all the while working as a RN on the COVID unit, God did the unthinkable. We were able to weather every storm, overcome every obstacle from the extreme delays from USCIS (United States Citizenship and Immigration Services) to the indefinite closures of embassies, airports, and the suspension of flights due to the pandemic. Despite everything we had gone through, all of the disappointments, God made it possible; and my husband was finally granted an interview months later. At that point, we were expecting things to run rather smoothly. We had thought that we had overcome all that we needed to and that our reunion was imminent. Much to our surprise, another huge unforeseen obstacle was about to steal the joy and hope that God had given us. On the day of my husband's interview at the Liberian embassy, he was told that he was denied the visa because all of his documents had been lost and that they had no idea what went wrong. Our whole world was shattered. How could such a thing happen? How was this even possible? This was a rare occurrence. How could this have happened to my husband? Those were the thoughts that ran through my mind. I was emotionally and physically exhausted. I had lost all strength in me to cry, pray, or do anything. I had rendered myself helpless without even having the strength to call on the name of God. With the little strength I had gathered, I began with research and was devastated after finding out that the process and the wait period could be as long as six weeks to two years until documents were recovered, not to mention the possibility that we would have had to begin the process from start. I was discouraged and defeated. But with the prayers and encouragement of my family and friends, something rose up in me, and I began to trust God. I began to decree and declare that my husband was not going to miss another birthday of our daughter. He was not going to miss another Christmas or another wedding anniversary. I called my husband that same night, and we prayed together. We bombarded the atmosphere and stood on the word of God and the promises that he has for our life. We reminded him of those promises. The next morning when we woke up, my husband had a different attitude. He told me that he trusted that God would change our story, and I agreed and proceeded with my day. I made calls to my state representative and the Liberian embassy, all the while still believing and trusting in God for a miracle. Before that day ended, my husband received a call from the Liberian embassy stating that they had retrieved his documents and that he was to report to the embassy the next day to pick up his visa.

Two weeks later, my husband arrived to the United States of America. Glory be to God. In a situation that seemed bleak, where nothing made sense and man couldn't help us, God stepped in and turned our situation around. There is nothing that is too difficult for the God that we serve. I will continue to testify to the goodness of God, for he is God and God alone, and He gets all the glory.

Ms. Charline Abraham
(Medical Student)

I'll spread my wings, and I'll learn how to fly. I'll do what it takes until I touch the sky. Or I'll do what it takes and not touch the sky? This has become an ongoing battle. Is it to do the work and get the results, or do the work and pray the outcome is what you hoped for? There are so many ways and versions to put this question, but I can say the outcome is always dependent on the plans that God has for your life. This fiery faith that we talk about, I believe it is merely dependent on what you believe God says about you. This fiery faith is sort of like being on a train and waiting to stop at your destination, but it never comes. However, you're supposed to keep the "faith" that eventually you will make it there. I say all of this to get to me…I mean I am still struggling every day to keep the faith, and although when things do not go the way I plan, it is always for my greater good. I can't help sometimes but to question God. My life is nothing short of a miracle. The way moments have intertwined is simply, again by faith. In fact, I can't write just one moment where I've had fiery faith because honestly, it's a journey. I can't say at any moment of my life when I really wanted something that I wholeheartedly said this is going to happen for me. It's the little moments of reminding myself who God is through my trials and tribulations that makes the difference. Some people make it look so easy, and it's easier said than done, but even up to this day, my "fiery faith" comes in spurts. In the moments when my faith has to be the strongest, I am reminded by the devil that it is not possible. This can be looked at in a bad way, but when this happens to me, I quickly surrender to God and stand firm in his word, and this is truly when it all matters. Being in medical school especially, I feel like there are always doubts. The devil, the world, and people have always made me feel as if I am not enough; so I have challenged each obstacles when it's shown itself. I know this is supposed to be about a moment where I've had fiery faith, but I specifically cannot pick one. The Lord has been too good to me every day. I have to remind myself to have faith so this "fiery faith" we talk about in my case is needed every single day. So the question again is, Is it do the work and get the results, or do the work and pray the outcome is what you hoped for? I believe the answer to my own question is, ask God for direction before you even start the work and give it your all, and if it is the outcome that you prayed for, God gets the glory, and if it's not the outcome that you prayed for, God still gets the glory. I will continue to spread my wings and learn how to fly and do what it takes until I touch the sky because with faith, it is truly possible.

Anonymous

The definition of *fiery*: consisting of fire or burning strongly and brightly. The definition of *faith*: complete trust or confidence in someone or something. In August 2022, my cell phone rang, and I could see it was my doctor's office. I answered the phone and thought I'd hear the nurse on the other end, but to my surprise, it was my physician.

He said, "Hi, this is Dr. Catastrophic. Is this a good time to talk? I have the results of your second mammogram and biopsy."

As I listened to the cheerless tone in his voice, I knew, whatever he was about to utter, was going to be disturbing.

The doctor stated, "I'm not going to call you into the office, you need to know now, so we can start fighting this."

In that moment, my heart started racing violently fast.

He asked me to sit down and then said, "There is no easy way to say this. I'm sorry, you have breast cancer, stage 3."

I felt like someone just bashed me in my stomach with a battering ram. I couldn't breathe correctly. I felt winded. I had to make myself inhale and exhale slowly. I didn't respond. I just listened to what the doctor was saying and listened to his suggested medical advice. When we hung up the phone, I just looked out the window, into the trees, and stared at the picturesque sea of green leaves. For a moment, I thought, I'm not ready to leave this magnificent earth. Look at the stunning cerulean sky and the sun that shined so radiantly. Is this all coming to an end? Do I have an earthly future? I looked at the sky and said, "Lord, if this is your will, then this is your will." I couldn't cry. I couldn't do anything for a moment. I was in shock. All I could do is stare out the window. Cancer, me, *wow*. What is going on? Then, I remembered my Bible and the verse Exodus 20:12, "Honour thy father and thy mother, that thy days may be long upon the land which the Lord thy God giveth thee." I honored my father and mother. What was happening? Well, in my mind, at age fifty-six, I felt I haven't lived long enough. And the Lord promised, if you honored your father and mother, your days will be long on this earth. At that moment, I prayed and believed that this was not it for me. I have a lengthy and bright future. Then, of course, after praying, I had to Google everything the doctor voiced, especially after he told me not to Google. Research was saying complete removal of both breasts. My PCC did say I would have surgery, maybe radiation. He said there are many options in 2022. He also said the oncologist would let me know further steps when I met with her. I took a deep breath and decided well I wouldn't have to wear a bra anymore. I had to think of something positive.

Four days later, I met with the oncologist, I asked God for strength before I went in. And within twenty minutes, my whole world changed. My blessing had occurred. The oncologist asked me to explain what I was told. She wanted to make sure I understood the whole process, in its entirety. I started speaking and giving her details of my understanding.

"I was told, you have stage 3 breast cancer, right breast."

She immediately stopped me and said, "No, wait, who told you that? That is wrong!"

I was confused, and she was mad at the misinformation that was conveyed to me. She started asking me questions and jotted down every word I was saying. Her head shook from left to right in disbelief, and she began to speak.

"You have stage 1 breast cancer, and I worked at Dana Farber for ten years, prior to working here, and you will be fine."

I was dazed! It says in Matthew 17:20–21, "For truly I tell you, if you have faith the size of a mustard seed, you will say to this mountain, move from here to there, and it will move; and nothing will be impossible for you."

I knew that God made this earth in seven days. I knew that God parted the Red Sea. I knew that Jesus fed thousands with five loaves and two fish. I knew that God did not allow Daniel to be eaten in the lion's den. In Daniel 3: 23–27, Shadrach, Meshach, and Abednego did not get burned in the fiery furnace. They didn't even smell like smoke. God is Almighty. He is everlasting. In the Bible, when God makes promises, he doesn't break them. Isaiah 41:10, "Do not fear: I am with you; do not be anxious: I am your God. I will strengthen you; I will help you; I will uphold you with my victorious right hand." So, I held on to God's word very tightly, and still do. Two weeks later, I had surgery, lumpectomy, and my right breast only. I also had one lymph node removed to check for any spread of cancer.

Results: lymph node were completely clear, no spread of cancer, no chemotherapy would be needed.

Amen and Hallelujah. One month after removal, I had eleven weeks of radiation every day, Monday through Friday, right breast only. Now I have to take a pill every day for the next ten years. The Lord has blessed me undeniably. I am highly supported and favored! Exodus 20:12, because I honored my father and mother, my days will be long on this earth. I talked to God, on my knees in prayer, and explained that I felt the ages of ninety to one hundred would be long in my eyes, but with my full mental clarity, of course. The Lord wants us to be specific. Nothing is impossible. Proverbs 3:5, "Trust in the Lord with all thine heart and lean not unto thine own understanding." Sometimes, the Lord allows us to walk through challenging times. He never said it would be easy. He will never give you more than you can handle, and he will walk you through, if you have faith and belief. God allows good and tough times for a reason, and you have to trust and believe he has a plan for everything. Just trust God. Give your heart to the Lord.

I was a Christian prior to cancer, and I love God even more after cancer. I talk to God daily, all throughout the day. I read daily morning scripture, and this summer I will be rebaptized, because I was baptized when I was twelve years old and want to rededicate myself to the Lord. The best part of my day is my two-hour ride home after work. That time is used to listen to Joel Osteen and Tony Evans, to hear God's word and reset my mind every day, because this world is tough, and the devil is like a roaring lion seeking who he may devour. The fight is real. Ephesians 6:11, "Put on the whole armour of God, that ye may be able to stand against the wiles of the devil." Lastly, John 3:16, For God so loved the world, that he gave his only begotten Son, that whosoever believeth in him should not perish, but have everlasting life." He sent his *only* son so we could all go to heaven. Think about it for a moment. How many of you would send your only son to die? I'm sure, no one is raising their hand. That is how much God loves us. Can I get an Amen? Thank you, Father, Thank you, Lord. My faith comes from reading his Word and knowing beyond a shadow of a doubt that he loves me.

Ms. Lorpu Faijue
(A mother)

My life story was not an easy one, but the small mustard seed of faith my mother planted in me as I grew up became my anchor during difficult times. I come from one of the poorest countries in the world, despite its wealth of natural resources. Corruption and the failure to properly utilize these resources have projected my country as impoverished. Many parents, including my own, were often forced to give their children to other family members to care for due to lack of adequate income or the inability to provide basic needs.

In 1990, while living with my uncle, I had a boyfriend, as any young girl might. My uncle did not approve of my relationship and gave me an ultimatum to either leave his home or end the relationship. Believing that my relationship was healthy and beneficial, I chose to stay with my boyfriend, which resulted in my uncle removing me from his home. Two years later, I had my first child. Despite the country's dire conditions and my own inadequacies in caring for a child, I held onto the belief that something good would come of my life.

I was often told that I would not succeed in life, yet I refused to let negative thoughts overtake me. I kept the faith, relying on the support of others to help care for my child. When my daughter was six years old, an opportunity arose for her to go to the United States with distant family members from her father's side. Trusting in my faith and feeling led by God, I agreed to let her go, despite the uncertainty of ever seeing her again. Faith, to me, is the evidence of things unseen and unknown, and I took action on the parts I could control.

In 2001, I received the news that my daughter had arrived in the United States at the age of eight. I prayed and continued to live, believing that one day we would be reunited. My relationship with my boyfriend ended, and I eventually married someone else, with whom I had three amazing children. Throughout it all, I never lost hope, and my faith continued to grow.

In 2019, I reunited with my daughter in the United States for her college graduation. I am now a US citizen, and all of my children are doing well, with my son serving in the US Navy. This book, "Fiery Faith," is a testament to the power of faith, Author by the daughter I knew God will manifest himself. You see this all began with one decision to stand by what I believe in and act on it, despite my daughter's father and I not working out, the seed that was planted has brought forth a great fruit. But without God it would not have turned out as well as it did. In our faith journeys we all need God the creator. This is what changed my story for the better. This is the only guaranteed to a successful outcome. My story of faith has not only shaped my life but also impacted many others.

Thought—Belief—Faith—Action—Results = POWER

October 28, 2024
6:15 a.m.–6:18 a.m.

The Full Story: You Have The Full Story

While reading Exodus 30:1–10.

The scripture describes the instructions that were given to Moses regarding burning incense and what Aaron was to do. Here is what the Holy Spirit told me:

> You see those who serve and practice these things now because they truly believe they are serving God. What makes those who believes in Jesus Christ special is that you have the full story. Others have a piece of the story, some of the story, half of the story but you have been given the full story. The Holy Spirit is part of the full story, Christ is part of the full story, the Father is the full story.
>
> What people believe is what they will put into action and will defend it strongly, despite the lack of it being the whole, if they believe in the half they will defend it. It takes a special individual to be open to receiving another addition to their belief, not forsaken their truth yet knowing that there may be more to complete it and make it *the whole truth.*
>
> *Faith is walking by and in the whole truth, seen or unseen.* Without the whole truth, it remains at belief. Belief can be altered. *Faith…true faith remains unhinged, becomes actions.*
>
> Your faith as a Christian, a believer in the Kingdom of God must be in the full story. Yet the judgment of those who do not believe in the full story and rather being okay with the half truth, part of the truth I will

deal with that. My grace is different in how I see my creation versus how my creation sees each other.

You have the full story

Keep moving in it

Doing greater works than I have done while on the earth. As I live, so shall you.

There is a story about a woman who was bleeding for twelve years and got healed.

Mark 5:24–34:

So Jesus went with him. A large crowd followed and pressed around him. And a woman was there who had been subject to bleeding for twelve years. She had suffered a great deal under the care of many doctors and had spent all she had, yet instead of getting better, she grew worse. When she heard about Jesus, she came up behind him in the crowd and touched his cloak, because she thought, "If I just touch his clothes, I will be healed." Immediately, her bleeding stopped, and she felt in her body that she was freed from her suffering.

At once Jesus realized that power had gone out from him. He turned around in the crowd and asked, "Who touched my clothes?"

"You see the people crowding against you," his disciples answered, "and yet you can ask, 'Who touched me?'"

But Jesus kept looking around to see who had done it. Then the woman, knowing what had happened to her, came and fell at his feet and, trembling with fear, told him the whole truth. He said to her, "Daughter, your faith has healed you. Go in peace and be freed from your suffering."

Thought—Belief—Faith—Action—Results = POWER

A thoughts led to believe, which led to faith in action steps of touching of the cloak, to the results of healing and finally being in contact with Power (and or receiving power).

Which phase are you currently in?

What is preventing you from moving to the next?

As we moved further, verse 34, "Daughter your faith has healed you. Go in peace and be freed from your suffering.

It's important to ask this question to oneself, has my lack of faith in action kept me in bondage to my suffering?

Final Faith Exercise
Congratulations!

Why practice faith at the point of need when people become desperate when you can begin to naturally practice faith now, as you have heard about these solutions are guaranteed from God as the true source. We have reached a point where it is your choice, think over these final questions.

- Can your source be defeated by you?
- Can your source be defeated by men?
- Can your source fit in the compact of the human mind?
- Can your source only be touched by human hands?
- Can your source be defeated by another source... GOD?

> If you declare with your mouth, "Jesus is Lord," and believe in your heart that God raised him from the dead, you will be saved. For it is with your heart that you believe and are justified, and it is with your mouth that you profess your faith and are saved. As Scripture says, "Anyone who believes in him will never be put to shame." For there is no difference between Jew and Gentile—the same Lord is Lord of all and richly blesses all who call on him, for, "Everyone who calls on the name of the Lord will be saved." (Romans 10:9–13 NIV)

If you have read to this point, *congratulations*! You have received an incline of a faith seed. Now to receive the best results of personal revelations and deeper results, you must align with a source nobody can take away from you. So, if you believe with your heart, confess these words with your mouth to accept this source into your life. This should not be something that you are conjured to do, allow it to come from your heart.

> **Dear Lord Jesus Christ, I know that I am a sinner, and I ask for Your forgiveness. I believe you died for my sins and rose from the dead. I turn from my sins and invite You to come into my heart and life. I want to trust and follow You as my Lord and Savior. I believe and have faith in you, now and forever.**

Congratulations! Look at that, you're Crazy after all! Welcome to the undefeated source of fiery faith team!

In the Bible, there is a template of prayer that people of God are taught to pray. Within this prayer Jesus teaches us to say "Thy will be done on earth as it is in heaven"

Thy will be done on earth as it is in heaven. It has been revealed to me;
This is in two accounts, may God's will be done in the Earth you walk on as it is in Heaven.

Secondly as we are Created out of heaven (our spirits) and are formed from the Earth (our flesh)
May God's will be done and made perfect in our flesh as it is perfect in our spirit. As you have surrendered your life to Jesus Christ, In your next journey as a person of Fiery Faith. Welcome back to the Kingdom of God where you belong. Go and live in unapologetically Crazy Faith…. wait….*Fiery Faith!*

"Nevertheless when the Son of man cometh, shall he find faith on the earth?" –Luke 18:8

Reference

Author's Message:

Cambridge English Dictionary. "Faith." https://dictionary.cambridge.org/us/dictionary/english/faith.

Grace Theological Seminary. "What Does Faith Mean?" https://seminary.grace.edu/what-does-faith-mean/.

Chapter 1:

The Holy Bible, New International Version (2011). "Mark 9:23–24." Grand Rapids, MI: Zondervan.

Harvard Medical School. "Faith and Healing." Accessed February 25, 2023, https://hms.harvard.edu/news/faith-healing

The Britannica Dictionary. "Crazy." Accessed March 9, 2023. https://www.britannica.com/dictionary/crazy

Cambridge English Dictionary. "Crazy." Accessed March 9, 2023, from https://dictionary.cambridge.org/us/dictionary/english/crazy.

Bible Gateway. "Isaiah 7:9." Accessed March 2023. https://www.biblegateway.com/passage/?search=Isaiah+7%3A9&version=NIV

Chapter 2:

eBible. "What Is the Significance of the Seraphim Bringing the Burning Coal from the Altar to the Writer in Isaiah 6:6." Accessed February 25, 2023, from https://ebible.com/questions/21087-what-is-the-significance-of-the-seraphim-bringing-the-burning-coal-from-the-altar-to-the-writer-in-isaiah-6-6.

Chapter 6:

Epoch Inspired Staff Time. "Excuse Me, Sir, Do You Sell God?: Little Boy and His Bottle of 'God's Kiss"

www.ingramcontent.com/pod-product-compliance
Lightning Source LLC
Chambersburg PA
CBHW031651040426
42453CB00006B/272